D0947021

UNDERSTANDING
PHILIP K. DICK

Understanding Contemporary American Literature
Matthew J. Bruccoli, Series Editor

Volumes on

Edward Albee • Sherman Alexie • Nicholson Baker • John Barth
Donald Barthelme • The Beats • Thomas Berger
The Black Mountain Poets • Robert Bly • T. C. Boyle • Raymond Carver
Fred Chappell • Chicano Literature • Contemporary American Drama
Contemporary American Horror Fiction
Contemporary American Literary Theory
Contemporary American Science Fiction, 1926–1970
Contemporary American Science Fiction, 1970–2000
Contemporary Chicana Literature • Robert Coover • Philip K. Dick
James Dickey • E. L. Doctorow • Rita Dove • John Gardner
George Garrett • John Hawkes • Joseph Heller • Lillian Hellman
Beth Henley • John Irving • Randall Jarrell • Charles Johnson
Adrienne Kennedy • William Kennedy • Jack Kerouac • Jamaica Kincaid
Tony Kushner • Ursula K. Le Guin • Denise Levertov
Bernard Malamud • Bobbie Ann Mason • Cormac McCarthy
Jill McCorkle • Carson McCullers • W. S. Merwin • Arthur Miller
Lorrie Moore • Toni Morrison's Fiction • Vladimir Nabokov
Gloria Naylor • Joyce Carol Oates • Tim O'Brien • Flannery O'Connor
Cynthia Ozick • Walker Percy • Katherine Anne Porter
Richard Powers • Reynolds Price • Annie Proulx
Thomas Pynchon • Theodore Roethke • Philip Roth
May Sarton • Hubert Selby, Jr. • Mary Lee Settle • Neil Simon
Isaac Bashevis Singer • Jane Smiley • Gary Snyder
William Stafford • Anne Tyler • Gerald Vizenor • Kurt Vonnegut
David Foster Wallace • Robert Penn Warren • James Welch
Eudora Welty • Tennessee Williams • August Wilson • Charles Wright

UNDERSTANDING
PHILIP K.
DICK

Eric Carl Link

The University of South Carolina Press

9/13/10
Lan
$ 39.95

© 2010 University of South Carolina

Published by the University of South Carolina Press
Columbia, South Carolina 29208

www.sc.edu/uscpress

Manufactured in the United States of America

19 18 17 16 15 14 13 12 11 10   10 9 8 7 6 5 4 3 2 1

Library of Congress Cataloging-in-Publication Data

Link, Eric Carl.
  Understanding Philip K. Dick / Eric Carl Link.
    p. cm. — (Understanding contemporary American literature)
  Includes bibliographical references and index.
  ISBN 978-1-57003-855-6 (cloth : alk. paper)
  1. Dick, Philip K.—Criticism and interpretation. 2. Science fiction,
 American—History and criticism. I. Title.
  PS3554.I3Z745 2010
  813.54—dc22

                                                        2009028390

For Laura

Contents

Series Editor's Preface

The volumes of *Understanding Contemporary American Literature* have been planned as guides or companions for students as well as good nonacademic readers. The editor and publisher perceive a need for these volumes because much of the influential contemporary literature makes special demands. Uninitiated readers encounter difficulty in approaching works that depart from the traditional forms and techniques of prose and poetry. Literature relies on conventions, but the conventions keep evolving; new writers form their own conventions—which in time may become familiar. Put simply, *UCAL* provides instruction in how to read certain contemporary writers—identifying and explicating their material, themes, use of language, point of view, structures, symbolism, and responses to experience.

The word *understanding* in the titles was deliberately chosen. Many willing readers lack an adequate understanding of how contemporary literature works; that is, what the author is attempting to express and the means by which it is conveyed. Although the criticism and analysis in the series have been aimed at a level of general accessibility, these introductory volumes are meant to be applied in conjunction with the works they cover. They do not provide a substitute for the works and authors they introduce, but rather prepare the reader for more profitable literary experiences.

M. J. B.

Preface

Much has been written about Philip K. Dick, and the scholarly attention he has received, coupled with the post–*Blade Runner* fascination Hollywood has shown for Dick's work, has made him both a cultural phenomenon and one of the most celebrated writers of science fiction in the twentieth century. The recent publication of two volumes of Dick's best novels in the famed Library of America series has offered Dick, at least symbolically, a well-deserved spot among the pantheon of America's best writers.

The purpose of the present volume is to offer an introduction to the work of this prolific, strange, unforgettable, and utterly unique American author. It is intended to serve as a point of entry for critical inquiry into Dick's life and work, as well as a useful companion for the reader of Dick's work. It is largely a synthetic work: it attempts, at least in part, to present an overview of what has been written about Dick during the past fifty years. To be sure, much truly fine criticism has been written about certain of Dick's novels from nuanced critical standpoints—Marxist critics have, in particular, produced some very provocative readings of Dick's works—and these treatments of Dick's works are noted throughout the study. But the intention of this volume is not to advance, validate, or invalidate any of these more focused, thesis-driven, specialized studies. Instead, this volume has been written to introduce readers to some of Dick's key themes and to guide readers toward a fuller appreciation of his literary achievements.

Dick's commentators have the task of deciding which works to cover and which to leave out of a study. With a writer as prolific as Dick, this is no easy task, and those who choose to write about Dick are always open to the charge of having overlooked a key text or given short shrift to someone's favorite story or novel. This is a particularly difficult thing to negotiate in a book of this size, where space is at a premium. There has been no attempt in this study to cover Dick's entire canon: a few of Dick's works receive no commentary at all, and some texts that deserve fuller treatment are passed over much too quickly. In an effort to provide a study that could profitably accompany any reader of Philip K. Dick, regardless of how much or how little or in what capacity one has read Dick's works, this study focuses largely on themes in Dick's works and on the shape and structure of his career as a writer. Extended treatments of six of Dick's works are grouped together in the final chapter of this study, but even these readings are but introductions to rich novels that could easily support closer reading and deeper analysis. The reader of this study who is interested in works by Dick not covered in this study, or who wants to delve deeper into the criticism of this complex author, is encouraged to consult the selected bibliography at the end of the study. This bibliography, although not exhaustive, is comprehensive, and all of the major critical statements are annotated.

CHAPTER 1

Understanding Philip K. Dick

In an interview given in 1981, just a year before he died, Philip K. Dick recalled a documentary he had seen in the 1960s on the plight of the Galapagos turtles. The documentary detailed how the turtles, and their vulnerable offspring, were killed wholesale by a variety of predators. One female turtle, as the documentary chronicles, after laying her eggs, got turned around and instead of heading back to the security of the ocean began to crawl inland. As the turtle inched farther and farther inland, she began to dehydrate in the sun. As the filmmakers followed the doomed turtle, she gradually slowed her pace, and the motion of her flippers changed from a crawl to a swim. Despite being farther from the ocean than she had likely ever been, and on the verge of certain death, the turtle thought she was in the ocean.

Dick was horrified, not only that the turtles were at their most vulnerable and subject to slaughter during the most important moment of their lives, the moment when they lay their eggs and provide for a new generation of sea turtles, but also at the tragic fate of the misdirected turtle, caught in a web of illusion as it exhausts the last of its energy and dies. As Dick noted in the interview, never had he had such a "sense of awfulness" as at that moment.[1]

That night, as Dick lay in bed, a voice woke him. The voice explained to him that the turtle would find its way back to the ocean—at least, as far as the turtle knew. The voice said that the turtle had been supplied an alternate reality—a subjective reality—in which she truly believed she was in the ocean swimming freely. In the comforting light of this benevolent vision, the cruel fate of an inland death vanished for the turtle. The story Dick relates of the turtle is telling, and it reflects themes that would interest him throughout his thirty-year career as an author: the nature of subjective experience, the individual caught between shifting realities, the tragic and awful struggles of life, the irony of heading blithely in the wrong direction, the horror and pity of death. Even the voice Dick heard in the night—the moment of contact between the human and the transcendent—is an issue he returned to again and again in his novels and short stories. Whether in an interview or in an essay, when Philip K. Dick reveals he heard a voice talking to him in the still of the night, he is not necessarily speaking metaphorically. He may not understand how or why the voice has manifested itself to him, but he is generally sure *he heard a voice.*

This anecdote is not the key to understanding Philip K. Dick; he is far too complex and multifaceted to be illuminated so simply. But the story of the turtle serves as a point of entry into the life and career of a man who some have claimed to be the greatest science fiction writer of the twentieth century. Whether the greatest or not, Dick is undeniably one of the most provocative, experimental, and challenging; he is a prolific writer who broke the rules of a genre and whose influence and importance—always admitted—seem to grow greater each year as a new generation of readers and critics comes to terms with the significance of his achievements within the field of science fiction and within twentieth-century American literary history.

Philip K. Dick's life was as provocative, as disturbing, and as filled with the uneasy juxtaposition of mundane events, all-too-human failings, and profound mysteries as his novels.[2] He was born in Chicago on December 16, 1928, to Joseph Edgar Dick and Dorothy Kindred Dick. Philip was the elder of a pair of twins. His twin sister, Jane, died a mere six weeks later. There is reason to suspect that Jane was undernourished and was not given proper and timely care by Edgar and Dorothy. The death of his twin—although he was too young to comprehend it at the time—would, in later years, haunt Philip, and even into his forties and fifties one finds him reflecting with great sorrow and bitterness on the loss. A few months after Jane's death, the Dick family relocated briefly to Johnstown, Colorado, and then a month or two later to the San Francisco Bay area. In 1933 Philip's parents divorced. Philip remained with his mother while Edgar moved to Reno, and from 1935 until their return to Berkeley in 1938, Philip and Dorothy lived in Washington, D.C.

Dick began writing short stories while still attending public school in the Bay Area. A music fan, during his teens he held part-time jobs in two record stores, each catering to different musical tastes, and his knowledge of music, especially classical music, already great, continued to grow. The numerous allusions to music (both classical and popular) in his novels and short stories reflect this keen interest. During his high school years, Dick struggled with agoraphobia and other—primarily psychological—ailments, and received some psychotherapy in order to help him through this challenging time. In 1947 Dick enrolled in the University of California at Berkeley, but dropped out after only a few weeks. The reasons for the swift exit from school are uncertain, but likely had something to do with his unwillingness to participate in the Reserve Officers' Training Corps (ROTC) program. The following year Dick married Jeanette Marlin. The marriage, which lasted only a few months, would prove to be the shortest of Dick's five marriages (and, perhaps because of its brevity, it is the union his biographers know least about) His second marriage, to Kleo Apostolides, in 1950 would prove more successful. The couple bought a small house in Berkeley, and Dick worked for a time in a record store. He also began to attend a series of writing workshops conducted by the science fiction writer and publisher Anthony Boucher, who encouraged Dick in his writing and bought his short story "Roog" in 1951. This marked his first sale, and inaugurated a thirty-year career as a writer. In 1952 Dick became a client of the Scott Meredith Literary Agency—a relationship that would last throughout his life—and, leaving his job at the record store, he set out to write full time. His first story to appear in print, "Beyond Lies the Wub," appeared in the pulp magazine *Planet Stories* in 1952.

During the early years of his writing career, Dick focused on short science fiction stories, which sold quickly to pulp magazines but earned him very little income. He also wrote the occasional mainstream novel, none of which were accepted for publication at the time, and only one of which, *Confessions of a Crap Artist* (written [w.] 1959, published [p.] 1975), was published in his lifetime By the middle of the 1950s, however, Dick, although still consumed with writing a growing stack of unpublished mainstream novels, turned the remainder of his energies away from short stories and toward science fiction novels. These science fiction novels found the success his mainstream novels did not. His first published science fiction novel, *Solar Lottery,* appeared in 1955.

Dick's life, already psychologically complicated by his penchant for phobias, his therapy sessions, the loss of his sister, his parents' divorce, a strained relationship with a headstrong mother, and a short, failed first marriage, became even more complex. In the early 1950s he began to take amphetamines to treat his phobias—and soon thereafter as a means to fuel a physically taxing writing schedule. In addition, his phobias were rein-forced by an encounter with Federal Bureau of Investigation (FBI) agents, who sought to recruit Dick and Kleo to relocate and report on student activities—presumably anti-American activities—at the University of Mexico. Dick and Kleo turned down the offer, but the recruitment visit by the FBI left a mark on Dick and fed his anxieties about government surveillance. These anxieties, fueled by a number of other incidents in later years, remained with him the rest of his life, and are reflected in many of his novels.[3]

Dick's marriage to Kleo lasted until 1958, when he met Anne Rubenstein, a widow with three young girls. Kleo and Dick divorced, and Anne and Dick were married in 1959. The follow-ing year they had a daughter, Laura Archer Dick. During the 1950s Dick's science fiction stories, then novels, including such solid efforts as *Eye in the Sky* (1957) and *Time Out of Joint* (1959), were published, but his mainstream novels found no out-lets, and by the end of the decade Dick, tired and frustrated, was ready to walk away from the business, which he did briefly from late 1960 to early 1961. He spent those months helping his wife, Anne, with her custom jewelry business, but he soon found that the life of a jewelry designer was not for him, and he returned to writing, drafting and publishing his Hugo Award–winning *The Man in the High Castle* in 1962. The success of *High Castle* gave Dick the motivation he needed to renew his efforts, and he set aside his hope for mainstream success in order to focus full time on writing science fiction. During the next two years he would pen a dozen novels, including such masterpieces of the genre as *Martian Time-Slip* (w. 1962, p. 1964), *Dr. Bloodmoney, or How We Got Along after the Bomb* (w. 1963, p. 1965), and *The Three Stigmata of Palmer Eldritch* (w. 1964, p. 1965). Despite these triumphs, Dick's economic and marital woes continued, and his marriage to Anne ended with separation in 1964 and divorce in 1965. The following year Dick married his fourth wife, Nancy Hackett, and with her had a second child, a daughter, Isolde, in 1967. The late 1960s also proved productive, and Dick produced, among a host of other works, his well-known *Do Androids Dream of Electric Sheep?* (w. 1966, p. 1968; the novel became the basis for the movie *Blade Runner*) and the masterful *Ubik* (w. 1966, p. 1969). But in 1970 his marriage to Nancy ended in divorce, and Dick's life grew increasingly chaotic as he delved deeper into the drug counterculture of the late 1960s and early 1970s. A mysterious break-in in his home in 1971, still unsolved, added to Dick's increasing fear, depression, and anxiety—culminating, ultimately, in a failed suicide attempt in Vancouver in 1972.

Following his suicide attempt, Dick was admitted to X-Kalay, a drug treatment facility, and a modestly cleaner Dick moved to Fullerton, California, in April 1972. Having befriended a professor at the University of California at Fullerton, Dick would sell his papers to the Special Collections department of the university library (where his papers reside currently). In 1973 Dick married Leslie ("Tessa") Busby, his fifth and final wife (although this marriage also ended in divorce in 1976). The couple would have a son, Christopher Kenneth Dick, in 1973. The marriage to Tessa rejuvenated Dick, and after a two-year hiatus he began to write again, working on his dark masterpiece about the underbelly of the California drug culture, *A Scanner Darkly*, which was eventually published in 1977. He also published *Flow My Tears, the Policeman Said* in 1974 (it had been written primarily in 1970), which won the John W. Campbell Award for best science fiction novel of the year.

In February and March 1974 Dick had a series of powerful mystical visions, and he began to keep a journal in an effort to record, explore, and explain these experiences. He called this journal, which he worked on for most of the remainder of his life, the *Exegesis* It would eventually run to some two million words. The failure of his marriage to Tessa in 1976 resulted in a second failed suicide attempt. Despite his battles with anxiety and depression, and his numerous failed marriages (as well as a host of failed romances with other women), the late 1970s did see Dick's economic straits finally turn around as royalties from reprint editions of his works, foreign sales, and movie options (especially the option on *Androids* for the movie *Blade Runner*) began to afford Dick some much needed freedom from constant financial anxiety. His writing production—if one does not count the *Exegesis*—slowed during the late 1970s, but with the turn of the decade he wrote and published three final novels, two of which—*VALIS* (1981) and *The Transmigration of Timothy Archer* (published posthumously in 1982)—are among his best. He died on March 2, 1982, of heart failure following a series of strokes, and his ashes are buried next to those of his twin sister, Jane, in Fort Morgan, Colorado. Now, in his honor, the Philip K. Dick Award, sponsored by the Philadelphia Science Fiction Society with the support of the Philip K. Dick Trust, is given each year to the best original paperback novel in the field of science fiction.

This brief biographical sketch records only some of the significant dates and names associated with Dick's life. Important as these facts are, and as influential as the events of his life were upon his writings—Dick drew liberally and unashamedly upon the events in his own life, whether joyous, tragic, or mysterious—they only tell one piece of a much larger story. Dick was a voracious consumer of ideas and a lover of philosophy. There was a restless quality to Dick's mind. He would entertain all ideas, and reject them all just as easily, seeming to find more satisfaction in the perpetual quest for explanations of the philosophical dilemmas of human life than in the explanations themselves. He would embrace a theory—about God, about politics, about science, about anything—turn it on a spit in his mind until it was thoroughly cooked, then declare it overdone and toss it aside. Dick was intellectually driven, and his intellectual curiosity is reflected not only in the provocative treatments of complex philosophical themes in his works but also in the vast array of references one finds in his works to obscure and arcane knowledge from both Eastern and Western history. Although Dick rarely demonstrates his scholarly pursuits with the highbrow sophistication of a modernist text such as T. S. Eliot's "The Waste Land," he does in many works—and especially in his later novels of the early 1980s—display the playfully encyclopedic curiosity of postmodern authors like Thomas Pynchon. Dick once noted that the wide-ranging influences of the contemporary science fiction writer should include journals that "deal in the most advanced research of clinical psychology, especially the work of the European existential analysis school"—as well as studies of C. G. Jung, Zen Buddhism, and Taoism—and "really authoritative" historical studies. In addition, the writer should read "Medieval works, especially dealing with crafts, such as glass blowing—and science, alchemy, religion, etc. Greek philosophy, Roman literature of every sort. Persian religious texts. Renaissance studies on the theory of art. German dramatic writings of the Romantic Period" (*Shifting Realities* 64–65).

This wide-ranging intellectual curiosity had a direct impact on his writing. One thing that distinguishes Dick's work from much of the other narrative writing appearing month after month in the pulp magazines of the mid-twentieth century is its engagement with philosophical and theological ideas. In the midst of the psionic powers, aliens, space ships, and other paraphernalia of the genre, one finds Dick exploring pre-Socratic philosophy, world religions, and the epistemological theories of Descartes and Hume. Dick was no ivory tower intellectual, however, and his novels and short stories are as much about life in the United States in the mid-twentieth century as they are about arcane philosophical and theological concepts.

In his work Dick responded to the climate of his times. In the 1950s, when Dick first turned his talents to serious writing, one can find clear reflections of the post–World War II era of cold war politics, atomic scares, bomb shelters, and McCarthyism. In the 1960s Dick's work is heavily influenced by the Berkeley counterculture scene. Many of Dick's best works from the 1960s directly engage the issue of drugs and drug culture, sometimes as metaphor and symbol, other times as tangible and tragic. One also finds Dick working out implications of the civil rights movement, the rise of the Black Panther Party, the shadowy activities of the Central Intelligence Agency (CIA), and the host of other social issues that the youth counterculture and the Beats gravitated to in their protests and writings. In the early 1970s Dick was enraged by Watergate, disenchanted with the outcomes of 1960s drug experimentation by the stoner youth culture in California, and disturbed—along with the nation—with the implications of the Vietnam War and its aftermath.

Right up to the end of his life, Dick responded in his writing and in numerous interviews given during his last few years to the climate in America during the Carter and early Reagan administrations. To read the work of Philip K. Dick is not only to read of the future but also to read a version of the history of U.S. culture throughout the entire cold war era. And he frames this history—both future and contemporary—in the conventions of pulp-era science fiction as well as in the deepest mysteries of world philosophy.

CHAPTER 2

Philip K. Dick, Novelist of Ideas

One of Dick's greatest literary frustrations was his inability to break into the mainstream market as a writer of novels of social realism. Throughout the 1950s Dick wrote numerous non–science fiction novels (as many as a dozen, although several of them are no longer extant), but none of them were accepted for publication. The dating of Dick's novels is imprecise, but evidence suggests that his earliest mainstream effort—predating any of his science fiction novels and stories—was *Gather Yourselves Together* (w. 1950). This work was followed by *Voices from the Street* (w. 1952–53), *Mary and the Giant* (w. 1953–55), *The Broken Bubble* (w. 1956), *Puttering About in a Small Land* (w. 1957), *In Milton Lumky Territory* (w. 1958), *Confessions of a Crap Artist* (w. 1959), *The Man Whose Teeth Were All Exactly Alike* (w. 1960), and *Humpty Dumpty in Oakland* (w. 1960). It was not until a small press brought out an edition of *Confessions of a Crap Artist* in 1975 that one of these works appeared in print, and not until the appearance of his final novel, *The Transmigration of Timothy Archer,* published shortly after his death in 1982, that Dick finally produced a novel that is both mainstream and ranks among his finest works—although *Transmigration* has so much in common with Dick's other late theological novels, *VALIS* and *The Divine Invasion,* that, in context, it hardly stands out from the pack as a particularly *mainstream* work. Nevertheless, with the rise of interest in Dick in the 1980s, all of Dick's realist novels have found their way into print (except, of course, for the three novels no longer extant—*A Time for George Stavros, Pilgrims on the Hill,* and *Nicholas and the Higs*).[1] During this same period, from 1950 until 1960, Dick wrote more than eighty short stories and eight science fiction novels, a level of productivity he would maintain, except for a few brief interludes, throughout the rest of his career.

Several of the realist novels from the 1950s are forgettable, and even his best effort—*Confessions of a Crap Artist*—cannot match the level of aesthetic or philosophical interest generated by his science fiction masterpieces. Even Dick's better science fiction novels from the 1950s—*Eye in the Sky* and *Time Out of Joint,* both written during the same period as the mainstream works—have generated far more attention from critics and readers than any of the mainstream novels. Certainly when reading one of Dick's realist works one is acutely aware that it is a Philip K. Dick novel. The tone, the use of dialogue, the anxieties of the main characters, and the narrative voice are all readily identifiable. But the lack of imaginative restraint that Dick employs in his science fiction works is absent in the more reserved mainstream novels, and, at least in the opinion of some critics, the works suffer accordingly. The mainstream novels are geared much more toward character development as opposed to plot and incident manipulation, and they lack, to a degree, the humor and the playful element of surprise that characterize the complex plotting of masterpieces such as *The Three Stigmata of Palmer Eldritch* and *Ubik.* Moreover the mainstream novels of the 1950s do not exhibit to the same extent the unbridled metaphysical musings of *VALIS* and *The Divine Invasion.* This is not to suggest that the mainstream works are humorless or that they do not demonstrate any of the metaphysical issues that manifest themselves in Dick's science fiction novels, but the tone of the mainstream novels is often muted and dark, and the extravagant intellectual gymnastics of the science fiction novels of the mid-1960s and early 1980s is restrained in the realist novels.[2]

Yet for all of this, the realist novels are not without their interest and merit, and there are flashes of greater things to come in some of them. Moreover, as an index to Dick's growth as a writer during the apprenticeship decade of the 1950s, one does find in the mainstream novels the development of some of the key narrative strategies and character types that appear throughout the rest of his body of work. As Kim Stanley Robinson has noted, these key elements of Dick's style can be found right from the beginning: "The various character types that reappear so frequently in Dick's novels are almost all in *Voices from the Street*: the hapless protagonist, leaving his unimportant job and losing track of reality; the protagonist's boss, forced by business interests to harm the protagonist in some way; the protagonist's apathetic and clinging wife; a dangerous, intense young woman, both attractive and repellent; and a mysterious cryptic religious leader" (Robinson 5). As a group, the mainstream novels concern troubled relationships, broken marriages, extramarital affairs, failed businessmen, manipulative women, violent flare-ups, and weary characters struggling to find their way among the detritus of 1950s American culture.[3] To one degree or another, these all-too-human concerns remain central in Dick's work throughout his long and prolific career.

Most of these characteristics are descriptive of Dick's *Confessions of a Crap Artist*. The "crap artist" of the title—Jack Isodore—is one of Dick's more unusual and well-drawn characters. He is alienated from society, is emotionally stunted, and spends his time accumulating odd and arcane bits of knowledge, which he can process "scientifically" in order to give order and shape to his life. His psychological peculiarities make it impossible for him to function normally in society, and although not mentally challenged, he is treated as such by his family. His sister, Fay Hume, another strongly drawn character, is manipulative, foul-mouthed, and sexually aggressive, and uses those around her for her own benefit. Her husband, Charley Hume, has neither the intellectual ability to defeat Fay at her own game nor the detachment of Jack that would allow him to smile in the midst of heartbreaking turmoil. Fed up with Fay's manipulation, his outlet is violence, and at the end of the novel he slaughters all of the family animals, attempts to kill Fay, but fails, and winds up committing suicide. Added to this mix of psychologically troubled—even damaged—individuals are Nathan and Gwen Anteil, whose new marriage is broken through extramarital affairs between Nathan and Fay and between Gwen and a neighbor.

The most unusual feature of *Confessions* is the shifting narrative point of view, a technique Dick would use throughout many of his best novels. Some of the chapters are told from the first-person point of view of Jack, others from the first-person point of view of Fay, and still others from third-person limited-omniscient points of view from the vantages of Charley and Nathan. The effect of shifting from chapter to chapter between these four points of view is to complicate any effort on the part of the reader to fix responsibility or place blame for the tragedies of the novel. Even the least sympathetic character, Fay, is seen in a more humane and sympathetic light in the chapters narrated from her point of view (though not in regards to her treatment of Jack, and her opinion of children—she describes the average child as a "filthy amoral animal"—is hardly going to win her mother-of-the-year awards). The horrors perpetrated by Charley both early (when he strikes Fay for manipulating him into the embarrassment of purchasing feminine hygiene products for her) and late (his slaughter of the animals and suicide) in the novel, when read against the manipulations of Fay and the weak-willed immorality of Nathan, are given at least some sympathetic psychological motivation. Dick once suggested in an interview that *Confessions* was in part influenced by his reading of the American modernist author Nathanael West. Indeed the blend of grotesque characters floating through a haze of violence, extreme and bizarre behavior, and ambiguous morality that one finds in such works as *Day of the Locust* and *Miss Lonelyhearts* does bear some resemblance to what one finds in *Confessions.*[4]

Throughout *Confessions* the character of Jack Isodore (of Seville, California) attracts the most attention and is the most sympathetic. His name is an allusion to Isodore Seville, the seventh-century author of an encyclopedia of the world's knowledge that ran to some twenty volumes. Fay, who has little love or understanding to offer her brother, Jack, throughout the novel (her husband, Charley, offers the most kindness to Jack), finds that Jack's "brain simply had a warp to it, that in distinguishing fact from fiction he chose fiction, and between good sense and foolishness he preferred foolishness. . . . Like some creep in the Middle Ages memorizing all that absurd St. Thomas Aquinas system about the universe, that creaky, false structure that finally collapsed—except for little intellectual swamp-like areas, such as in my brother's brain" (38). Yet in the tradition of the fool in *King Lear* and Pip in *Moby-Dick,* Jack's perspective on events— while unabashedly naive—is often acute in its assessments and telling in its critique. For instance, when, in his discussion of the hollow-earth theory (Jack believes that the earth is hollow and whole civilizations live within it) he notes that at any moment "the ground may open up beneath our feet, and strange and mysterious races may pour out into our very midst. . . . Every time there's a quake I ask myself: is this going to open up the crack in the ground that finally reveals the world inside?" his enthusiasm for a crackpot theory not only foreshadows the emotional earthquake of events to come in the novel but also, metaphorically, serves as a critique of 1950s America: beneath the beehive hairdos and wholesome television entertainment of 1950s America, what shadowy worlds reside? In *Confessions* the American pastoral of Marin County, California, is revealed to be a world of adultery, domestic violence, dark psychological manipulation, end-of-the-world cultists, and unapologetic self-ishness and greed. As Jack concludes at the end of the novel, the "whole world is full of nuts. It's enough to get you down" (245).

In the end *Confessions,* as with many of Dick's other main-stream works, is, in the words of Charley Hume, about "the breakdown of relationships between living things" (55), a senti-ment that not only reflects on the breakdown of causality dis-cussed by the philosopher David Hume (to whom Charley and Fay's last name alludes) but also refers in a broader sense to the chaos of modern American relationships. Dick would treat this subject extensively in his science fiction novels as well.

Philip K. Dick: Science Fiction Writer

Dick stipulated that there were some key differences between the mainstream novel and the science fiction novel. To its credit, Dick believed, the mainstream novel tended to delve deeper into the nature of interpersonal relationships than did the science fic-tion novel, but the science fiction novel, to its credit, tended to engage purely intellectual concepts in a manner not easily dupli-cated by the mainstream novel. Moreover science fiction, Dick claimed, is freed from the burden of "style as such but can range farther in terms of its content." But, Dick notes to his chagrin, science fiction tends to be written more with the shallow optimism of youth who have not yet "suffered at the hands of life." The mainstream novel—quality literary fiction, presumably—deals "with the defeated," with "those who have lost the first bloom" (*Shifting Realities* 64). To be sure, Dick's own mainstream efforts deal with the defeated and with suffering, but his contrary claim about science fiction, while true in some cases, has its notable exceptions, as Dick's own science fiction novels bear witness. If Dick believed that science fiction in America lacked the strength to deal with suffering and human defeat, he set out to change the intellectual and social landscape of science fiction with his own writings.

With its roots in a long tradition of utopian and dystopian writing, in eighteenth-century *conte philosophiques,* in the early-nineteenth-century gothic romance, and in the fantastic voyage tales of Jules Verne in the late nineteenth century, science fiction emerged as one of the dominant narrative genres of the twentieth century. In terms of its impact on the culture at large, one might make the case that science fiction is *the* central narrative genre of the twentieth century, especially in the United States. Paradoxically science fiction is one of easiest genres to recognize, yet like so many other literary genres, attempts to define it have proven difficult. Much of this difficulty arises from the fact that science fiction has so much in common with fantasy literature, on the one hand, and postmodern fiction, on the other. Undoubtedly any attempt to define science fiction must, at some level, account for its relationship with fantasy literature. Moreover one observes—with the clarity that comes from a historical perspective only now coming into focus—science fiction may be (and may have been all along) the most postmodern of postmodern literatures, with its clear and direct responses to new developments in science (particularly to new issues in quantum mechanics and cosmology), to postindustrial-age theories of artistic creation, to new theories in linguistics and language theory, as well as to mid-to-late-twentieth-century concerns with the decentering and fragmentation of personal identity—issues Dick dealt with throughout his career.[5]

Science fiction is often characterized by an easily recognizable set of features, conventions, and scenarios, and Dick made liberal use of them in his short stories and novels. Alien encounters (whether hostile or benign) are one of the key conventions of the genre, as are scenarios built around the colonization of other worlds. Alternative history scenarios are common in science fiction—and this forms the basis of Dick's *The Man in the High Castle*—as are narratives built around time travel, dying Earths, lost civilizations, discoveries and inventions (including robots, androids, and extravagant technological devices of all kinds), evolutionary developments, and all manner of fantastic voyages. Thematically science fiction has proven as wide-ranging and free in its intellectual pursuits as any other genre; yet, as a genre, science fiction has found six different thematic orientations particularly provocative: the relationship between technology and humanity, ecology and the environment, the nature of *otherness*, issues in philosophy and theology, the nature of human sociopolitical systems, and the implications of evolution (both progressive and regressive) on human biological and social systems. Reading science fiction is a unique enterprise, for, more than any other genre, the language of science fiction possesses a high degree of what science fiction author and critic Samuel R. Delany has called "subjunctivity." That is, in science fiction there is a high degree of tension between the words that comprise the narrative and the things to which the words refer. This subjunctivity is often produced by the literalization of metaphor: in a science fiction story, when a character says, *"My world exploded around me,"* the character might mean that literally. This subjunctive tension—this shift from the figurative to the literal—is one of the hallmarks of science fiction and makes reading science fiction a unique—and uniquely entertaining—experience.

In their attempts to define science fiction over the years, some critics and writers have abandoned the term *science fiction* and adopted the term *speculative fiction* instead. Speculative narratives might be defined as those that seek to discover or explore, by means of some form of speculative activity (projection, extrapolation, experimentation, hypothesizing) something about the human condition and the nature of reality. Defined in this manner, the term *speculative fiction,* in time, may indeed prove more useful for critics, but the term *science fiction* is so embedded in literary culture that one suspects it will never be completely abandoned. As something of a compromise, many critics and authors are choosing the acronym SF to refer to works by Dick and others, for it may stand for either term, and Dick himself often used this acronym to refer to his and his fellow writers' fiction.

Among many useful attempts to define science fiction—or SF—the one Darko Suvin offers proves fertile when discussing Dick's works. Suvin writes that science fiction is "a literary genre whose necessary and sufficient conditions are the presence and interaction of estrangement and cognition, and whose main formal device is an imaginative framework alternative to the author's empirical environment."[6] Cognition implies the use of the human capacity for reason to analyze a situation, while estrangement implies that the world of the narrative is defamiliarized in some capacity. In other words Suvin suggests that science fiction is a form of literature that not only makes us see ourselves and our environment in new ways through the depiction of unfamiliar events, objects, and environments but also provokes in the reader a desire to understand the principles that govern these unfamiliar things.

Central to Suvin's definition is the concept of the *novum* (plural *nova*). A key ingredient of science fiction is the incorporation of a *novum,* a "new thing," a feature that separates the world of the narrative from our empirical environment. For Dick, the notion of *novum* as a new idea (as opposed to a new thing) is key. "What a SF story really requires is the *initial premise* which cuts it off entirely from our present world."[7] The world of science fiction, according to Dick, must be different from the experiential world of the author in "at least one way," and that way must give rise to fictional events that "could not occur in our society—or in any known society present or past. There must be a coherent idea involved in this dislocation; that is, the dislocation must be a conceptual one, not merely a trivial or a bizarre one—*this* is the essence of science fiction, the conceptual dislocation within the society so that as a result a new society is generated in the author's mind, transferred to paper, and from paper it occurs as a convulsive shock in the reader's mind, *the shock of dysrecognition.*"[8] This "shock of dysrecognition" parallels the concept of estrangement as articulated by Suvin.

The presence of the *novum* distinguishes science fiction and fantasy from realistic narratives, but it also can help one distinguish between science fiction (in which the *novum* is natural—a rational extrapolation of known things, for instance) and fantasy (in which the *novum* is *super*natural). This distinction does not always correlate with what one finds in any given work of science fiction or fantasy, but it is useful as a general guideline. One thing Dick believes that separates fantasy from science fiction rests in his claim that science fiction is not—when done right—escapist literature. It is not concerned with giving its readers a means to avoid the grim realities of the modern world; it deals with reality in fundamental ways.[9] The science fiction author (hack writers excepted, of course) begins always with the question "What if . . . ?" and allows the answer to that question to unfold in the written word. It is a literature rooted in "possibilities, not actualities," but they are possibilities grounded first in reality.[10] Part scientist, part political activist, and part artist, the science fiction author breaks the grip waking reality has on the reader—not completely, but in part—and places the reader in a neutral territory, a "third space," that is neither fully concrete nor fully abstract, but which is "connected to both and hence relevant."[11] The science fiction writer, Dick argues, is "able to dissolve the normal absolute quality that the objects (our actual environment, our daily routine) have." Still, he or she does not sever the bond entirely, but keeps one foot firmly entrenched in the real.[12]

As a science fiction writer in the 1950s keeping one foot in the realities of the American sociopolitical climate, Dick dealt with the culture of cold war paranoia, intimations of governmental surveillance and conspiracy, Communist and anti-American witch hunts, and the rise of television-era mass media marketing. As a whole, it seemed a bleak picture to Dick, and he believed that the socially responsible science fiction author of the time had to face up to the grimness of the vision. In a 1955 essay called "Pessimism in Science Fiction," Dick notes that "all responsible writers, to some degree, have become involuntary criers of doom, because doom is in the wind; but science fiction writers more so, since science fiction has always been a protest medium. In science fiction, a writer is not merely inclined to act out the Cassandra role; he is absolutely obliged to."[13] The problem with the doom story, Dick points out, is that there is really only one—the story of war, in which cold war tensions have their climax and denouement. In contrast, there are an infinite variety of "bright successful, nondoom futures" that might be imagined, but to do this would be to evade a certain social responsibility on the part of the science fiction writer.[14] But despite the pessimism of these remarks, Dick's own fiction is neither confined to the limits of the doom story nor constrained within the boundaries of what he may have deemed socially responsible science fiction in 1955. The value of science fiction, for Dick, did not lay in its Cassandra role; it lay in its ability to grapple with the *new idea*. In response to a questionnaire in 1969, Dick wrote that the chief value of science fiction is to present "new ideas too difficult or too vague as yet to be presented as scientific fact (e.g. Psionics). And ideas that are not scientific fact, never will be, but that are fascinating conjectures—in other words, *possible* or alternate science systems. World views that we can't 'believe' in but that interest us."[15] Such is the project of Philip K. Dick: the pursuit of interesting alternative representations of reality and the exploration of the philosophical themes these alternate realities reveal.

Philip K. Dick: Postmodernist

As noted in the previous section, there is a bond between science fiction—particularly post–Golden Age science fiction (that is, post 1930s and 1940s)—and postmodern literature, and this bond is growing more apparent with increased critical hindsight.[16] Granted, science fiction seems more or less postmodern depending on whose theory of postmodernism one uses to define the movement. Nevertheless, while acknowledging at the outset that the ongoing debates over the definition and cultural meaning of postmodernism cannot be settled here, one can still make the general observation that Dick's science fiction novels illustrate almost every defining characteristic of postmodernism.[17] Indeed were Dick not segregated from other important writers of the second half of the twentieth century by means of the label *science fiction writer,* novels such as *Ubik* and *VALIS* and *The Man in the High Castle* would stand next to the works of Pynchon, Vonnegut, Barth, and Calvino as demonstrably postmodern in theme and development, and likely as major achievements within the canon of postmodern literature. Certainly, when one entertains the theories of Jean Baudrillard and Frederic Jameson, one cannot help but think that their theories of postmodernism (influential as they are) were devised in part with a stack of Philip K. Dick novels at hand, or at least in mind. And, to be sure, both Baudrillard and Jameson wrote about Dick, and both used his texts to illustrate certain features of postmodern literature.

As one critic has noted, one of the central themes of postmodern art rests in the "response to the preoccupation of late capitalism with the fabrication, exchange and sale of images rather than artifacts; the commodification of culture."[18] The apotheosis of the *image*—of simulations or simulacra—over the *thing* is one characteristic of postmodernism (and is a preoccupation of Baudrillard in his work on postmodernism and science fiction). Thus, in the marketplace, there is a shift in postmodern culture from the consumption of things to the consumption of images and information. The shift in the culture of consumption results in the commodification of simulacra, and Baudrillard claims that a by-product of this commodification is a gradual erasure of things themselves.[19] One is caught in a network of representations of things, rather than the things themselves. Certainly if there is a poet of simulacra—or of the blurring border between the real and the imaginary—and an incisive commentator on human paranoia in the midst of the media-fueled global technocracy of late capitalism, it is Dick.[20] Indeed Jameson's delineation of postmodern culture as characterized by international capitalism, the ubiquitous marriage of media and marketplace, and the elevation of commodities—the products of the international marketplace—to the status of cultural icons, describes Dick's fictional environments well.[21] Throughout his career—but particularly from the 1960s—Dick's novels and stories expose and comment on the interpenetration of media and everyday life (*The Simulacra, The Penultimate Truth*) and the recasting of commodities as near-sacred relics (*Ubik, Do Androids Dream of Electric Sheep?* "Foster, You're Dead"). Add to this Dick's critique of the conspiracy-based paranoia created by a cold war military-industrial complex (*Eye in the Sky, Time Out of Joint*) and endless variations on the theme of the changing nature of reality itself, and it is clear that Dick reflects a midcentury shift toward postmodernism and that he is a notable commentator on postmodernity.

There is a strong correspondence, then, between postmodernism and the work of Philip K. Dick. Even if one rejects the view of global economic activity upon which a neo-Marxist reading of postmodernity is, at least in part, based, Dick's work still may be profitably discussed within the context of the postmodern literary movement in the United States that flourished from the 1950s to the 1980s. Philosophically considered, postmodernism rejects the notion that individuals have ready access to a verifiable external reality: the philosophical basis of realism, in other words, is either rejected outright or at least called into question. The question is asked: is there a "real" world outside of our own perceptions or outside of language itself? Epistemological uncertainty—that is, uncertainty about the nature and validity of human knowledge—is a defining characteristic of postmodernism and is reflected in the works of postmodern authors. Philip K. Dick is no exception to this rule.

In terms of their formal structure, one of the hallmarks of many postmodern literary works is their use of metafictional devices. In their rejection of linear narrative strategies and the skepticism they demonstrate of the concept of the *real*—an external reality separate from the subject that has its own ontological existence—postmodern texts often turn inward and examine their own fictionality.[22] As one critic has noted, Dick's themes "function self-reflexively to question the nature of writing itself. Indeed had Dick not so firmly grounded his novels in the traditions of genre SF, he would almost certainly have been seen as an important member of the metafictional movement of the 1960s."[23] Dick uses metafictional strategies in a number of works. For instance, he experiments in radical ways with metafictional strategies in *VALIS,* in which he not only inserts himself into the narrative but does so in typically Dickean grand fashion: he divides himself—or a version of himself—into two characters (Phil Dick and Horselover Fat) and inserts them into the narrative in a way that makes them both two characters and one character at the same time. In an early novel, *The Man in the High Castle,* the fictional alternative reality of the novel (an alternative reality in which the Axis powers won World War II and divided the United States as spoils of war) is undercut by a subversive novel-within-the-novel called *The Grasshopper Lies Heavy,* in which it is posited that the Allies won World War II.

But, to complicate things further, the version of reality presented in *The Grasshopper Lies Heavy* is not *real* history, but is only an approximation of it; thus both the nature of historical writing and the fictionality of all versions of history are emphasized, calling into question the reader's own perception of what is understood as *real* history.[24]

Another common feature of many postmodern texts—and one that separates the works of the modernists from the postmodernists—is the breakdown of the distinction between high and low culture. Again, one can find this characteristic in Dick's works.It is this very feature that adds to the distinctive "Dickean" narrative style, with its fast-paced blend of sometimes arcane philosophical and theological ideas with action-oriented, media-savvy, information-age sensibilities. In the novel *Ubik,* Dick deals with issues of theodicy and entropy; one also finds a character arguing with a coin-operated talking door. In the short story "Faith of Our Fathers," Dick offers a harrowing vision of the disturbingly evil forces underlying surface "reality," and he does this by having a character receive messages directly through the television while taking a presumably recreational drug. In fact one could make the argument that in choosing to deal with such an array of philosophical and theological themes in his works (in addition to their function as sociopolitical commentary) through the medium of science fiction, Dick once again "out-postmoderned" other postmodernists. Although science fiction as a genre (or, as it is often called, a subgenre) is not *subliterary* by any means, it is often, in some circles, viewed as such, and Dick understood this prejudice too well. Dick himself distinguished between science fiction and "mainstream" fiction and associated (to an extent, at any rate, but not completely) the latter with more serious intellectual pursuits. Thus, in effect, by using the popular "low-culture" medium of science fiction as he did, he brought postmodernism—and his critique of postmodernity—to an audience that writers such as Borges, Calvino, Barth, and Barthelme rarely reached. As a result, it is not a surprise to find, a generation later, that Dick's influence on contemporary American culture is measurably broader than most of his contemporary postmodernist authors.

If the postmodern hero is characterized as alienated, socially maladjusted, and solipsistic by nature or circumstance, then Dick's characters are models of the type. Confronted with enigmas in a perplexing universe, the postmodern protagonist is a study in psychological abnormality and philosophical ambiguity. Because of these tendencies in contemporary American fiction, numerous postmodern American authors write what one critic has referred to as "illness stories."[25] These works focus on "individual maladjustment to social roles, in which the protagonist has difficulty deciding whether he (or sometimes she) is insane or society itself is crazy." According to Richard Ohmann, these narratives reflect "the contradiction that existed in post-1945 U.S. society between the belief that society [had] resolved its basic problems . . . and the reality of continued social conflicts over work, the family, and other aspects of life."[26] The "illness story" is aptly descriptive of some of the most notable works of the 1960s and 1970s in America—Ken Kesey's *One Flew over the Cuckoo's Nest* (1962), Joseph Heller's *Catch-22* (1961), and Walker Percy's *Love in the Ruins* (1971). When read in the context of the "illness story," *VALIS, The Three Stigmata of Palmer Eldritch, A Scanner Darkly,* and other of Dick's works clearly bear a strong relationship to these works by Kesey, Heller, Percy, and others in the postmodern "illness story" tradition. The protagonists of Dick's novels deal with a host of psychological illnesses, from anxiety to schizophrenia to extreme identity loss. What is often unclear for these characters, however, is the extent to which their individual troubles are only within themselves, or if their troubles are really a reflection of the social environment in which they live. Perhaps they are actually quite sane, and it is society itself that has been driven mad through social and political tensions and fears. To answer these questions requires clarity of perception—a luxury not often enjoyed by Dick's characters caught up in conspiracies and driven by paranoia.

Novelist of Ideas

In an interview conducted in 1976, Dick was asked if his decision to write science fiction was deliberate: "Yes," he answered, "because there's more likelihood in science fiction for the expression of *pure ideas* than you find in other genres."[27] This pursuit of the expression of pure ideas, whether one considers Dick in any of his incarnations as mainstream novelist, science fiction novelist, or postmodernist, is the key to understanding Dick's work. He is at heart a novelist of ideas. The ideas that Dick returns to again and again in his work are often related to the central questions of metaphysics: they are questions one asks in a quest for ultimate, and possibly absolute, knowledge about the nature of the universe and the nature of humankind. Is there a God? If there is, what is God like? Is God benevolent or malevolent? What is the nature of the universe itself? What is *real*? Other ideas Dick pursues in his writings are epistemological in nature; that is, they question the reliability of human knowledge and one's ability to know about things, about oneself, and about one's environment. They ask the age-old question, what is truth? They ask how can we distinguish between truth and falsehood, between what is real and what is mere illusion? Dick stated, "In a certain literal sense ideas are alive."[28] Christopher Palmer has summed up some of Dick's range of interests in this way: Dick's novels

> are intensely social affairs. Their narratives consist of encounters, disputes, confrontations; betrayals, desertions, uneasy reconciliations; philosophical discussions about fundamental issues such as the nature of love or the putative drive to life—or death—that underlies existence; headlong meditations on the part of the point of view character, canvassing radical, dismaying possibilities. The context is always one of radical change and radical changeability, on every level from the condition of one's job or marriage to the state of the universe and the meaning and purposes of God (of some god or other, anyway).[29]

But what makes Dick's works even more compelling is his manner of blending this exploration of metaphysical and epistemological themes into narratives filled with the mundane paraphernalia of everyday reality, and to do so with a sense of humor that ranges from slapstick to deadpan to dark. In Dick's world the most profound mysteries of the universe and the most mundane problems of everyday life coincide and are dealt with during the daily lives of electricians, housewives, plumbers, jewelers, salespeople, marketing executives, tourists, and neighborhood children at play.[30] Science fiction novelist and critic Stanislaw Lem noted that "Dick seems to foresee a future in which abstract and highbrow dilemmas of academic philosophy will descend into the street so that every pedestrian will be forced to solve for himself such contradictory problems as 'objectivity' or 'subjectivity' because his life will depend upon the result." Unfortunately for them, Lem observes, in this philosophical fight for their lives, Dick's characters are "doomed to failure in advance."[31] Still, by bringing metaphysical and epistemological dilemmas into the street, Dick is not only able to give new color to some age-old philosophical and theological problems; he is also able to do so in a way that simultaneously critiques the culture of his time.

In Dick's work one's inability to distinguish the real from the unreal manifests itself in government conspiracy as well as in the drug counterculture. One's confrontation with malevolent cosmic forces—even with real metaphysical evil itself—is described in terms of capitalist enterprise as well as cold war paranoia. The problems generated by a Cartesian mind-body split and the solipsistic implications that result are represented in terms of schizophrenia, amnesia, fear, alienation, and human despair, and are as likely in the world of Philip K. Dick to lead to comic tales of human ingenuity as they are dark narratives of human desperation, violence, and death.

CHAPTER 3

The Craft and Career of Philip K. Dick

It is common to view Dick's career as passing through at least three, possibly four, distinct stages.[1] Critics and biographers attempting to study the evolution of Dick's career generally follow the order in which Dick composed his works—as best as can be determined—instead of the actual publication dates, for often his works were published years after they were composed, and not in the same order they were written. For instance, the first nonmainstream novel he composed was *Cosmic Puppets,* but his first science fiction novel to be published was *Solar Lottery,* in 1955. Moreover, for a variety of reasons—financial pressures, creative blocks, exhaustion—Dick's published novels were sometimes swiftly composed expansions of earlier works, or they were long-delayed coauthored efforts, such as his collaboration with Ray Nelson, *The Ganymede Takeover,* which was started in 1964 but not published until 1967, and his collaboration with Roger Zelazny, *Deus Irae,* which was started as early as 1964 but not completed and published until 1976.

Taking these discrepancies into account, the general consensus is that the first phase of Dick's career lasted from around 1950, when he first began to take up writing as a profession with his drafting of *Gather Yourselves Together,* to 1960, when he temporarily abandoned writing and took up work in his wife's jewelry business. This decade of Dick's career is characterized by three different literary pursuits: his unsuccessful bid to break into the mainstream market, his swift and remarkable success as a writer of stories for science fiction pulp magazines (Dick would publish nearly seventy short stories between 1953 and 1955, with another handful to follow during the remainder of the decade), and his first successes as a science fiction novelist. Before the end of 1960, eight science fiction novels by Dick would be published. But Dick's frustrations with finding a place in the mainstream market—coupled with exhaustion after what can only be described as a feverishly productive decade—led to a brief hiatus. In fact the final two science fiction novels published in this phase of his career—*Dr. Futurity* and *Vulcan's Hammer,* both published in 1960—are weak retreads of previously written short stories (composed as early as 1953) and are among Dick's least successful novels.

As Robinson notes in his study, the common denominator among many of Dick's earliest science fiction novels is that they all have to do with the overthrow of a dystopian state, and, unique among the rest of Dick's canon, in these earliest works the attempts are successful.[2] Dick's interests in these novels are in both social satire of the American sociopolitical system of the 1950s and metaphysical speculation about the duality of nature and the cosmic forces that operate above and beyond human control. As Carl Pagetti writes: "Dick's fiction in the 50's moves along the double track of civil commitment and metaphysical representation of the struggle for power and of a destiny that transcends the will of even the most powerful of men" (19). Of these two "tracks," in his first science fiction novel, *The Cosmic Puppets,* Dick is most interested in transcendent struggles and is comparatively less interested in social satire (at least when compared with his other novels of the 1950s).

Although not published until 1957, *The Cosmic Puppets,* written in 1953, was the first nonmainstream novel that Dick wrote. It is in many ways better described as a fantasy novel than a strictly science fiction novel, although like many of Dick's later works, the line between the two is never clearly marked. If one were to strip *The Cosmic Puppets* of the language of fantasy—to remove words such as *spell,* and *magic,* and *golems,* which typically signal a fantasy environment—then the novel would not be much more fantastic than more successful later novels such as *The Three Stigmata of Palmer Eldritch, Galactic Pot-Healer,* or *The Divine Invasion.* In these later works, by not relying on the language of fantasy to the degree found in *The Cosmic Puppets,* the fantastic elements are rendered in such a way that they do not seem to radically violate Dick's science fiction landscape—which, admittedly, is in general more infused with fantastic and supernatural elements than the science fiction of many of his peers.

The story of *The Cosmic Puppets* is rooted explicitly in Zoroastrian theology. Dick noted in an interview—in characteristically exaggerated fashion—that the research he did into the bitheistic, dualistic religion of Zoroastrianism for *Cosmic Puppets* was a "turning point in my life."[3] This interest in bitheism would influence many of his later works. In this novel the use of Zoroastrianism is explicit: the cosmic struggle within the novel is between the Zoroastrian gods of Ormazd (the creative force) and Ahriman (the destructive force). Ormazd's daughter, Armaiti, the goddess of devotion, also makes an appearance in the novel in the character of Mary. The novel's plot is built around what turns out to be one moment or minor action in the epic, seemingly endless struggle between Ormazd and Ahriman, between the forces of creation and destruction. The two gods have squared off against each other over the town of Millgate, and Ahriman has cast a spell over it, causing a false layer of reality to envelope the whole town. In a fit of nostalgia, the protagonist, Ted Barton, returns to Millgate, the town of his youth, and in doing so sets in motion a sequence of events that result in dispelling the illusory reality constructed by Ahriman and restoring the town to its previous—real—state. Of course it is a Dick novel, so Barton's wife leaves him during the course of the novel, but Barton's encounter with the idealized (and unattainable) beauty Armaiti—with her "cascades of black hair" (136)[4]—at the end of the novel compensates somewhat for the loss of his spouse.

The Cosmic Puppets introduces one of the dominant motifs throughout the Dick canon: the notion of layered reality. In this case the version of reality apprehended by most of the residents of Millgate is only an illusory facade covering a deeper reality. As is true throughout Dick's work, this "deeper" reality is the playground of cosmic forces and allegorical figures with explicitly theological and/or philosophical significance. Here the layering is a result of a war between Zoroastrian gods, but in other novels one finds reality layered as a means of sociopolitical control, as in *Time Out of Joint,* or layered because of a fracture in human psychology, as in *A Scanner Darkly, Now Wait for Last Year,* and other works. Overall *The Cosmic Puppets* is an entertaining novel, but not a particularly good one. It certainly exhibits the hallmarks of apprenticeship writing, and is far surpassed by many of Dick's later works. The plot thrums along at a good, pulp fiction pace, but the characterization is particularly weak, and the story itself is plagued by inconsistencies and logical gaps. Nevertheless in many ways it sets the table for what Dick would subsequently produce, and it is a stark declaration from the outset that Dick was profoundly interested in, and influenced by, theological themes and questions, including questions about the nature of humankind and the structure of the universe itself.

Despite *The Cosmic Puppets'* earlier composition, *Solar Lottery* (w. 1953–54, p. 1955) was Dick's first published science fiction novel. Although *Solar Lottery* is still a minor work in the Dick canon, in tone and style it is more suggestive of his later, more accomplished work of the 1960s than is *Cosmic Puppets*. Still, it is a novel that does not quite know what to make of itself, and even though the best of Dick's novels often seem as though they are about to burst at the seems under the pressure of their multidimensional plots, *Solar Lottery* does in fact buckle a bit under its own weight. It is, simply, a book that is not quite sure in what direction it wants to head, and, as a result, several of the novel's ideas and plot lines are underdeveloped. Thus the climactic confrontation between Berkeley and Eleanor, as well as the revelatory encounter with the holographic John Preston on Flame Disc, seems rushed at best and inexplicable at worst. Too much is lost in the shuffle of plots in this fast-paced adventure novel. One is certainly left wishing for a clearer understanding of the almost comically mysterious "bottle" game, and, in a similar vein, Dick could have made much greater use of game theory than he did. On the other hand, one is drawn to *Solar Lottery* because Dick, even at this early stage of his career, unabashedly introduces provocative, often complex ideas into what would otherwise be a forgettable—if entertaining—pulp fiction extravaganza.[5]

Nevertheless *Solar Lottery* is a leap forward from *Cosmic Puppets*. Within its fast-paced, action-oriented, and entangled plot a number of provocative themes emerge, as well as commentary on political systems and political intrigue. Two of the numerous ideas introduced in the novel predominate. First, as a commentary on the nature of the universe itself, *Solar Lottery* sets up a tension between viewing the universe as governed by chance and viewing the universe as subject to controlling forces. The freedom/necessity dichotomy is one of the central concerns of game theory, and the central intrigue of the novel—the attempted assassination of Leon Cartwright by recently removed quizmaster Reece Verrick—directly addresses this dichotomy.

The novel's second dominant theme concerns the nature of loyalty. This theme is introduced right at the outset as the reader is presented a socioeconomic system in which jobs are held and secured through a pledge system rooted in absolute loyalties. But the dimensions of loyalty addressed in the novel expand beyond mere indentured servitude in the economic sector. *Solar Lottery* explores the significance of the concept of loyalty in love relationships, marital relationships, friendships, political relationships, and spiritual relationships. One ultimately discovers in *Solar Lottery* that the bond of loyalty is often a mere surface illusion, covering layers of disloyalty between friends, political allies, marital partners, and spiritual leaders and their flocks. As the protagonist, Ted Bentley, observes halfway through the novel, loyalty is just a word used to deflect attention from human selfishness. At its core, society is driven by individuals struggling for personal gain and power: if the facade of loyalty were dropped, Bentley notes, true human drives would be revealed. As Bentley says, "It's one big scramble for the top. They're all struggling to get up there—and nothing is going to stand in their way. When all the cards are turned up, you'll see how little loyalty counts" (85).[6]

These two major concerns in *Solar Lottery* merge in the novel's interest in the ethical implications of a society torn between the poles of absolute randomness and artificial control systems imposed by P-Cards, loyalty oaths, and voluntary serfdom. At the end of the work, the human conscience is revealed as the mediator of value in such a society. The renewed value of the human conscience is achieved by shifting the loyalty system binding one person to another in a power relationship subject to abuse, to a system in which one is first and foremost loyal to oneself. If one takes the oath of loyalty not to another but to oneself, then one is morally obligated to bear responsibility for one's actions. As Bentley notes at the end of the novel, "I'm probably the first person who was ever under oath to himself. I'm both protector and serf at the same time. I have the power of life and death over myself." To which Cartwright responds: "It sounds like a good kind of oath, to me. You take full responsibility for protection and for carrying out the work. You have nobody to answer to but your own—conscience" (190–91).

Another of Dick's earliest science fiction novels, *The World Jones Made,* written just after *Solar Lottery* in 1954 and published in 1956, is an exposé of the virtues of philosophical relativism versus social, political, and moral absolutism. The basic philosophical question that this novel asks is whether society is better off under the direction of institutionalized relativism, or if society can better prosper within the stability provided by an absolutist worldview. The novel ends as it begins, with a small group of characters forced to take refuge in a biosphere because they are trapped on a world in which they cannot survive. Each group is left to wait until it can return to a world for which it is better suited. Both the relativist and the absolutist societies create these situations, suggesting that all institutionalized systems perform similar functions in society.

Dick's concern with the conflict between institutionalized belief systems—especially as manifested in oppressive and conspiratorial sociopolitical systems—is evident in *The Man Who Japed* (w. 1955, p. 1956) as well. A minor work in the Dick canon, *The Man Who Japed* is an entertaining examination of forced morality and the necessity of taking moral responsibility out of the hands of governments and returning it to individual members of a society. Of Dick's other science fiction novels of the 1950s, two stand out as early triumphs—*Eye in the Sky* (w. 1955, p. 1957) and *Time Out of Joint* (w. 1958, p. 1959)—and two—*Dr. Futurity* and *Vulcan's Hammer*—as forgettable retreads. As the decade drew to a close, Dick was ready for a break.[7]

The second phase of Dick's career begins in 1962 with the publication of his Hugo Award–winning *The Man in the High Castle*. This begins what is often referred to as Dick's "major phase" (or some variation thereof), a phase that would last until the drafting of *Flow My Tears, the Policeman Said* in 1970 (which would not be published until 1974). During this decade one finds Dick at the height of his productivity and power, producing (amid other less successful works) such notable novels as *Martian Time-Slip, Dr. Bloodmoney, or How We Got Along after the Bomb, The Three Stigmata of Palmer Eldritch, Do Androids Dream of Electric Sheep?* and *Ubik*. Occasionally critics will divide this decade of work into two phases, suggesting *Three Stigmata* as a dividing point and viewing the first half of the decade as generally more successful than the second half, but the growing appreciation over the years of *Ubik* and *Flow My Tears* makes any claim for a falling-off of Dick's skills in the second half of the decade a somewhat dubious assertion Regardless of whether one views this period as one phase or two, during this era one witnesses Dick's keenest examinations of the unsteady nature of reality and the shifting nature of human identity.

The final phase of Dick's career begins in 1974 as Dick—having had a profoundly intense series of mystical experiences early in the year—gave his full attention to the pursuit of primarily theological themes. During this final phase Dick wrote and published his darkest portrait of drug abuse and paranoia—*A Scanner Darkly* (w. 1973–75, p. 1977), drafted his *Exegesis*, and wrote his final four novels, all centrally concerned with theological issues: *Radio Free Albemuth* (w. 1976, p. 1985), *VALIS* (w. 1978, p. 1981), *The Divine Invasion* (w. 1980, p. 1981), and *The Transmigration of Timothy Archer* (w. 1981, p. 1982). *A Scanner Darkly*, although not published until 1977, is tied thematically to the work of the 1960s and reads as a coda on that period of Dick's career and life—if not to one segment of American culture itself. Setting aside *A Scanner Darkly*, in Dick's post-1974 work one is struck by the intensity of his quest after theological and philosophical answers to the spiritual mysteries defining his own life. These novels are personalized explorations of theological themes. Early works such as *Counter-Clock World* (w. 1965, p. 1967), *The Three Stigmata of Palmer Eldritch*, and *Galactic Pot-Healer* are firmly rooted in theological speculation, but not in the same intensely personal manner of the works of Dick's final phase.

By the time Dick penned his late theological novels, he was far removed from his humble beginnings.[8] His initial forays into the world of science fiction were written for, and published in, pulp magazines. These magazines—such as *Astounding, Startling Stories, Planet Stories, The Magazine of Fantasy and*

Science Fiction (which, under the editorship of Anthony Boucher, bought Dick's first short story, "Roog"), and a host of others—created a ready marketplace for science fiction authors and fed a fan base eager for the latest creations by their favorite authors. But these magazines, not necessarily known for the relentlessly high quality of the stories they published, paid very little, and authors like Dick were forced—if they wanted to make a living as a writer—to turn out dozens of stories each year just to pay the bills. And sometimes, as Dick's life attests, even the bills couldn't get paid. And yet despite the financial drawbacks and the hectic schedules writers had to adopt in order to survive, these pulp magazines allowed writers an outlet for their works, an outlet that they otherwise would not have had, and they allowed Dick an avenue for publication right from the beginning, which, because of the failure of his mainstream novels, was crucial.

During the time that Dick was establishing himself as a science fiction writer, a changing of the guard was about to commence in the field. And as with so many other innovations in the genre, Dick led the way. The new guard would not really define itself—as New Wave science fiction—until the 1960s, but its roots can be traced to the post–World War II writing of Dick and others.[9] New Wave science fiction was a reaction against the formulaic (and often thematically optimistic) "hard" science fiction of the Golden Age.[10] The New Wave turned its attention to experimental narrative forms, to a more self-consciously literary approach to style, and to a focus on the "soft" sciences of psychology and sociology. New Wave authors tended to treat more controversial subject matter than earlier authors, and they echoed the social concerns—particularly the counterculture concerns—of the 1960s generation. In fact the arc of Dick's career traces the arc of the New Wave movement itself, with its roots in the 1950s, its domination in the 1960s and 1970s, and its decline in influence in the 1980s as cyberpunk—which Dick, always on the cutting edge, is also given credit as helping to create—became the fashion.

The renewed interest among writers of the New Wave in aesthetics helped pave the way for the acceptance of science fiction within the annals of "artistic" literature. In terms of literary style, Dick is a distinctive writer. Dick is not a great stylist in the traditional sense—he is not regarded generally as a meticulous craftsman of finely turned phrases. As a writer just getting started in the early 1950s, Dick was heavily influenced by both pulp magazine fiction and the fast-paced adventure novels of A. E. Van Vogt and others; yet at the same time, Dick was also heavily influenced by the acknowledged literary masters of the nineteenth and early twentieth centuries such as Joyce and Thackeray. From Joyce and Thackeray, Dick learned about the importance of characterization and ways in which novels can explore the uncharted depths of human relationships. From Van Vogt and the pulp writers, Dick learned how to write science fiction. These influences helped shape Dick's writing, but, as a stylist, it was not long—by the end of the 1950s at the latest—that Dick had defined his own unmistakable literary style. Dick's style is a fast-paced, often comic blend of the wildly imaginative and the all-too recognizably human. There are no heroes in Dick's novels, only humans. Characters who save the world are reluctant to do so and are as likely to be worried about their failing marriage as they are the threat of global catastrophe.

Despite the distinctiveness of the Dick "style," and all of his other accomplishments in the annals of literary history, his style often receives the most criticism. In 1967 one critic outlined the "flaws" in Dick's fiction, identifying five key weaknesses in his body of work (at least as it was constituted in 1967): poorly written passages; overly sentimental scenes; illogical plots and characters; too many ideas, symbols, and plots crammed into each novel; and weak characterization with no principal focal point.[11] To be fair, several of these alleged flaws could be leveled at almost any writer, regardless of reputation. Another American original, Mark Twain, comes instantly to mind in this regard. Dick wrote over forty novels: in a body of work so extensive, one can find any kind of flaw one wishes. Several of these "flaws," however, may in fact not be flaws at all. Many of Dick's best works are characterized by complex and convoluted plots filled with surprises and extravagant imaginative devices, and in his presentation of ideas, especially in the later works, Dick creates tour de forces of intellectual gymnastics. For many readers, these elements are hardly flaws: they are among the most appealing features of Dick's narratives.

For all of this, this last criticism—Dick's weak characterization with no principal focal point—requires the most direct comment. One of the highlights, and most readily identifiable features, of Dick's narrative style is his use of what has been called his "multifoci" point of view. Much in the manner of Faulkner before him, Dick fragments his narrative point of view in many of his works. It is rare for a Dick novel to be told from beginning to end from the same point of view. His novels are often ensemble pieces, with multiple protagonists, each with chapters devoted to narration from his or her point of view. Unlike Faulkner, Dick does not often resort to stream of consciousness, but he does make heavy use of free-indirect discourse in which readers get to listen in as characters mentally sort through their issues and perceptions. Stated another way, the primary point of view in a Dick novel is a limited-omniscient third-person point of view, in which the character who is the focus of the limited-omniscience shifts from chapter to chapter. Sometimes, however, Dick will shift to the first-person point of view. One finds this, for example, in his late masterpiece *The Transmigration of Timothy Archer,* which is told entirely from the first-person point of view of Angel Archer. In some of his most radical experiments with point of view, Dick will not only shift focal character but also will shift from first-person to third-person limited-omniscient. One sees this used with considerable—albeit unsettling—effect in his mainstream novel *Confessions of a Crap Artist,* in which some of the chapters are told from the first-person point of view of the title character, Jack Isodore; other chapters from the first-person point of view of Jack's sister, Fay Hume; and still others from the third-person limited viewpoint of Charley Hume or Nathan Anteil.[12]

In terms of characterization, Dick offers a mixed bag of weakly and strongly drawn characters, and, accordingly, depth of characterization is a distinguishing trait of many of his better works, while lack of character depth is symptomatic of several of his lesser efforts. Characters often cited as particularly well developed include Nobusuke Tagomi in *The Man in the High Castle,* Fay Hume in *Confessions of a Crap Artist,* Leo Bulero in *The Three Stigmata of Palmer Eldritch,* Felix Buchman in *Flow My Tears, the Policeman Said,* and Angel Archer in *The Transmigration of Timothy Archer.* When stocking his novels with characters, Dick generally draws upon a few types, and he uses variations on these types throughout many of his works (with notable exceptions). These types include the powerful executive or boss figure, the relatively less powerful "little man" (about which more will be said later), the repairman, the aggressive but seductive female, the passive but manipulative female, and the child caught in a web of mystical experiences. Of these types, Dick has proven most vulnerable to criticism in regards to his creation of female characters. Female characters are not rare in Dick's works; indeed, they are major figures in nearly every novel Dick wrote, but they are—with few exceptions, such as the strongly drawn sympathetic portrait of Angel Archer in *Transmigration*—almost always unsympathetic characters.[13] Dick was aware of this tendency in his work, and even referred to it as the "evil woman problem" found in his writing.[14] With all of his own marital difficulties, there is plenty of biographical evidence to suggest why Dick might have drawn his female characters in primarily unsympathetic ways.[15] One type of female character found throughout Dick's canon is what critics—following Dick's lead—have called the "dark-haired girl" (although not all of the characters who fit this description are brunettes). The dark-haired girl is, for Dick, the ideal woman: she is the woman who provides comfort in the midst of the Sturm und Drang of life. She is often a man's refuge from a shrewish wife, though she is not without her own problems.[16]

Dick distinguished between writing short stories and novels in terms of character development, and although his novels are not entirely immune from weak characterization, it is in his short stories where one observes a consistent focus on incident over characterization. In a preface Dick composed for his short story collection *The Preserving Machine,* he wrote: "The difference between a short story and a novel comes to this: a short story may deal with a murder; a novel deals with the murderer, and his actions stem from a psyche which, if the writer knows his craft, he has previously presented."[17] This shift from incident to characterization in the shift from the short story to the novel is a hallmark of much narrative writing in general, and is certainly not unique to Dick's work. But what is true for others is true for Dick: one finds in the novels a deeper examination of the motivations that drive the incidents, as opposed to a bald presentation of the incidents themselves. These trends in narrative writing are relative, of course, and because Dick was groomed on the frenetically paced, incident-driven fiction of Van Vogt and his fellow pulp writers, it should come as no surprise that even Dick's more character-driven novels are heavy with plot and incident.

Published shortly after his death, Dick's final novel, *The Transmigration of Timothy Archer*, serves as a suitable capstone for his career—although it was not intended to be so. Not only is it a mainstream work—yet one that flows quite seamlessly from the science fiction novels that precede it—it is one of Dick's most successful blendings of incident and character, and it features Dick's most complex and well-drawn female character: the first-person narrator, Angel Archer. *Transmigration*, a "literary" novel in Dick's own eyes, is loosely based on the life of Bishop James Pike, who was a friend of Dick's.[18] Pike was notorious among the Catholic orthodoxy for his flirtations with esoteric theology and the occult, and *Transmigration* captures moments of Pike's life through the lens of the fictional Angel Archer. As much as it is a novel about Pike's literal and theological wanderings, it is even more so a study of the effects of loss and grief on Angel.[19] Dick described *Transmigration* as a "novel about the crushing effect of death on a very intelligent, sensitive young woman who really loved her friends very deeply. And in writing it I'm really exploring the subject of the effect of the death of someone that one loves very much. The loss of a loved one. And it changes you and you're dehumanized by it. That suffering does not ennoble. I've never really bought the idea that we are somehow better off for suffering" (Lee and Sauter 139).[20]

During the last year of his life, as he was drafting *Transmigration*, Dick's fortunes were on the rise. Director Ridley Scott was in production with *Blade Runner*, and Dick was at long last free from the burdens of poverty. Dick struggled to make ends meet throughout most of his long career, and it was only in his final few years that the combination of royalties, advances, and movie options afforded him what can be described as a truly comfortable living—although he was never wealthy. Posthumously, however, Dick's reputation rose, and through reprintings of his novels and numerous big-budget film productions of some of his novels and shorts stories—starting with the classic *Blade Runner* in 1982 and including more recent movies such as Steven Spielberg's *Minority Report* in 2002—his fame and influence have grown to the point where it may be claimed without any exaggeration that Dick is the science fiction writer who has had the single greatest impact on American popular culture. Just as important, however, is the fact that Dick's impact on both American literary history and on the genre of science fiction itself has proven to be not just remarkable but truly profound. Put in different terms, it is no longer necessary to refer to Philip K. Dick as a great *science fiction* writer: in terms of his impact on American culture, his importance in American literary history, and his undeniable accomplishments within the field of science fiction in particular, Philip K. Dick is a great *writer*.

CHAPTER 4

The Themes of Philip K. Dick

As a novelist of ideas, Dick found himself gravitating toward a particular set of themes—and variations on those themes—throughout his career. Dick recognized this consistency and identified the two principal questions that shaped his career: what is real and what is human? Dick's fiction explores a host of answers to these two questions, and these explorations manifest themselves in a wide-ranging but interconnected set of ideas and motifs.[1]

Epistemology and the Nature of Reality

More than simply writing narratives in which what is deemed real is revealed to be illusion, Dick uses his tales of the breakdown of reality as a means to discuss questions of epistemology and metaphysics: specifically, Dick suggests a division between objective reality and one's subjective perception of reality (which often diverge radically in Dick's world), and he also questions the ontological basis of reality itself. Certainly Dick's novels unsettle the reader. The deliberate withholding in some of his works of a baseline or ground-level reality—a "true" reality that provides stability as the reader attempts to sort through the shifting layers of the narrative—creates not only interpretive difficulties for the reader but also adds a degree of narrative complexity found less often in science fiction than in the experimental postmodern narratives of Borges, Calvino, and Nabokov. In fact in some of Dick's works—in accordance with certain implications of quantum mechanics, cybernetics, and poststructural language theory—reality is not just depicted as colored by subjective perception; instead reality is a construct that shapes itself based on the ideology of the subject.[2] When in Dick's novels reality begins to shift for one or more characters, the questions the characters ask turn metaphysical. One critic has referred to this as Dick's "appeal to metaphysics" and notes that Dick's characters "often react to the discovery of a breakdown in reality by attempting to find something or someone 'behind' phenomenal reality" (Fitting 95). In order to discover what lies "behind" (or beyond), Dick's characters become enmeshed in metaphysical dilemmas about the very nature of reality itself, and these dilemmas form the thematic basis of many of Dick's best novels, from *Eye in the Sky* to *Now Wait for Last Year*, and became a central concern in the late 1960s with such works as *The Three Stigmata of Palmer Eldritch*, *Ubik*, and *Flow My Tears, the Policeman Said*, which all feature, in different ways, a gradual erasure of external reality and a corresponding retreat into solipsism. Notably, although the treatments of this theme in his novels of the late 1960s represent the high point of Dick's development of the discrepancy between what is real and what is illusion—and the corresponding breakdown of external reality such a realization often entails—the germ of this idea was present right from Dick's very first short story, "Roog"—in which a dog sees the environment around it in a radically different way from humans[3]—and would remain a preoccupation until the very end of his career, as witnessed in two of his greatest short stories, "I Hope I Shall Arrive Soon" (1980) and "Rautavaara's Case" (1980).

Dick once suggested that a basic test that separates dream from reality is consensus: if more than one person sees the same thing, then that is an indication of its ontological stability.[4] But the situation as depicted in many of his novels is far more complex than this test might indicate, from the mass hallucination of his first novel, *Cosmic Puppets,* to the complete breakdown in consensus reality in *Eye in the Sky* and *The Three Stigmata of Palmer Eldritch.* Indeed in *Eye in the Sky,* his most intense treatment of the world-shaping power of individual subjectivity of the 1950s, Dick explores the possibility that an individual's perception of reality may have the power to shape the consensus view itself.[5] Influenced by the philosophical and psychological theories of Hume, Kant, Berkeley, and Jung, *Eye in the Sky* forces the reader to reexamine the nature of reality itself and to question the validity of one's perceptions of the external world.[6] More than this, however, *Eye in the Sky* uses these metaphysical musings as the basis for constructing a parable of sorts about the domination of political ideology. Written as a reaction to both the McCarthy witch hunts and the specter of Communism rising in the West, *Eye in the Sky* is a condemnation of the totalitarian state, whether it manifests itself in religion or in politics.[7] This fusion of the metaphysical and the political is common in Dick's canon, and in novels such as *The World Jones Made, The Simulacra,* and *The Penultimate Truth* one finds different versions of the notion of how outside forces shape and manipulate consensus sociopolitical ideology.

In a more sophisticated and descriptive treatment of the subject/object discrepancy, Dick spoke at times of the difference between the *idios kosmos* and the *koinos kosmos.* The most important statement Dick made on this difference was in a letter written in 1969 to the Australian periodical *SF Commentary.*[8] Noting the influence of both Immanuel Kant and the European existential psychologists, Dick suggests that "for each person there are two worlds, the *idios kosmos,* which is a *unique* private world, and the *koinos kosmos,* which literally means shared world." The essential epistemological dilemma that arises from the discrepancy between the private and shared worlds stems from the fact that "no person can tell which parts of his total worldview is *idios kosmos* and which is *koinos kosmos,* except by the achievement of a strong empathetic rapport with other people." In many of his books, Dick observes, the "protagonist is suffering from a breakdown of his *idios kosmos,*" and as it does so "the objective shared universe emerges more clearly . . . but it may be quite different from the *idios kosmos* which he is in the process of losing" (Gillespie 32). The *koinos kosmos* to which the protagonist is exposed is not often an Elysian field. Dick finds that the cosmic, archetypal forces that govern reality itself are as often evil—in the sense of true ontological evil—as good. The "archetypal and transcendental forces" that the pro-tagonist is exposed to are often too powerful to be compassed by human reason, and they can lead to self-doubt at best, psycho-logically devastating madness at worst. In light of new devel-opments in science and language theory in the mid-twentieth century, a layer of complexity not seen in Kant's own time reveals itself. In Dick's words: "What is new in our time is that we are beginning to see the plastic, trembling quality of the *koinos kosmos*—which scares us, its insubstantiality—and the more-than-mere-vapor quality of the hallucination."[9] If the *koinos kosmos* proves to be insubstantial—as having no onto-logical reality itself—then the *idios kosmos* is all there is, and solipsism is the result. Whether the *koinos kosmos* is real or not, what is true for the characters in Dick's fiction from *Cosmic Puppets* forward is that, as Dr. Meade says in that novel, quot-ing St. Paul, we see "through a glass, darkly"—darkened by our own subjectivity. Or, in the technological future of Philip K.

Dick, through *A Scanner Darkly.* To be sure, as Dick notes in his 1976 essay "Man, Android, and Machine," for "absolute reality to reveal itself, our categories of space-time experiences, our basic matrix through which we encounter the universe, must break down and then utterly collapse."[10]

Examples of Dick's use of this notion of conflict between the *idios kosmos* and *koinos kosmos* proliferate throughout his canon, as in, to cite one example, "The World She Wanted" (1953), in which a woman lays claim to a man's life, declaring that he lives in her particular world (her *idios kosmos*). In a twist ending, however, after the man grows tired of the self-centered woman, he rejects her from *his* particular world. A more interesting early treatment of this conflict can be found in "Jon's World" (1954), with its clear echoes of Platonic idealism. In this time-travel narrative, the protagonist—a man named Kastner—has a son—Jon—who has persistent visions of a bucolic, agrarian, philosophically reflective society, which bears the hallmarks of the ancient Greek academe of Plato. These visions are a far cry from the war-torn reality of Kastner's world. As a result, in order to cure his son of these fanciful visions, Kastner has his son lobotomized. Later Kastner travels back in time in an effort to prevent a past scientist from developing the technology of artificial intelligence that results in the long-standing war between the humans and the mechanized "claws" that has so devastated the Earth. The changes Kastner makes in the time continuum result in the manifestation of the bucolic world foreseen by Jon in his visions. Jon's visions, the story suggests, are of a "more real" reality (57)—an idealized reality reminiscent of Plato's *Republic* and bearing the metaphysical stamp of Plato's allegory of the cave. Kastner had Jon lobotomized because his son's individual view of external reality did not bear any relation to the shared view of reality held by the society in which Jon and Kastner live, but in a reversal at the end of the story, it becomes evident that Jon had gained mystical insight into an alternate future state of reality. Jon's "madness" is the madness of transcendent revelation and is reminiscent of the madness of Uriel in Emerson's poem of the same name and of Pip in *Moby-Dick*. And both of these characters have their philosophical roots in Neoplatonic epistemological theory.

In discussing one of his most successful novels of the 1950s, *Time Out of Joint,* Dick noted that the fake reality created for the benefit of the protagonist by a manipulative government eager to gain tactical advantage in a long-standing war was emblematic of much of his writing and embodied the core "premise of my entire corpus of writing, really. This is my underlying premise. And this is that the world that we experience is not the real world. It's as simple as that. The phenomenal world is not the real world, it's something other than the real world. It's either semi-real, or some kind of forgery."[11] As an entry point for discussing conflicts over the nature of reality in Dick's work, the terms *idios kosmos* and *koinos kosmos* are useful, but they do not tell the whole story, and the works themselves, particularly the work of the late 1960s, suggest epistemological dilemmas concerning the nature of reality that cannot be easily reduced to a conflict between *idios kosmos* and *koinos kosmos*. Speaking generally, however, the movement in Dick's work is so often inward, and the deeper one delves into the self, the less certain one is regarding the stability or even existence of the external world. It is a type of Cartesian solipsism, with all of the uneasy conclusions regarding the solidity and stability of the external world such solipsism suggests. Dick explores this inward movement, and the subsequent erasure of the *real,* in countless ways:

through alternative history, through schizophrenia and madness, through drugs (literal, symbolic, and metaphorical), and through a host of other devices.

Gnothi Seauton: Know Thyself

When Ted Barton, the protagonist of Dick's first science fiction novel, *The Cosmic Puppets,* enters his boyhood town of Millgate only to discover that the town is completely different from how he remembered it, and that according to town records, he died of scarlet fever eighteen years earlier, he wonders if he has been caught throughout his entire life in a network of false memories and a false sense of identity. Ted wonders, "If he wasn't Ted Barton—*then who was he?*" (17).

As difficult as it is to know what is *real* in Dick's world, how much tougher is it to know the *self?* The words inscribed above the Oracle at Delphi in ancient Greece, *Gnothi Seauton* (know thyself), suggest another major theme in Dick's works. As one turns his or her attention away from the shimmering, translucent nature of external reality and looks inward, one is confronted with yet another epistemological crisis: can one know one's own self? Are memories a reliable source of information about self-identity? The uncertain nature of knowledge, often coupled with hallucinations caused by drugs, psychosis, or a variety of external forces, destabilizes the notion of personal identity in Dick's works. As a result, Dick's works are littered with characters who experience a crisis in self-identity of one sort or another, culminating in the late masterpieces *Do Androids Dream of Electric Sheep?* in which identity is undercut through planted memories; *Flow My Tears, the Policeman Said,* in which identity is completely erased; *A Scanner Darkly,* in which drug use has led to a schizophrenic psychological split; and *VALIS,* in which identity is intentionally divided by the protagonist—and, metafictionally, by the author—in order to come to terms with the implications of transcendent insight.

Implanted memories are a particularly easy way, in Dick's world, to cast doubt on personal identity. For the individual with false memories, a "fake" or manipulated sense of reality is the result: the relationship between the individual and his or her environment is revealed to be a mere construction, with no basis in epistemological certainty. One well-known example of this kind of epistemological crisis appears in "Imposter" (1953). According to Dick, this was his first story on the topic of "Am I Human? Or am I just programmed to believe I am Human?"[12] Here the protagonist, Spence Olham, is an android (with, the reader discovers, an explosive device contained within its chest capable of destroying the entire planet—which it does at the end of the story) that believes it is human (having had the memories of the now-dead human Spence Olham implanted in its circuitry).[13] One also finds Dick experimenting with the notion of a man unknown to himself in his entertaining story "Paycheck" (1952). In this fast-paced narrative, a man is hired to perform a secret job, a job so sensitive that all memory of the time spent performing the work is wiped from his memory upon completion of the contract. In the story the protagonist has to use a series of clues that he deliberately left for himself in order to reconstruct events that transpired during the period erased from his memory.

In another of his best-known stories, "We Can Remember It for You Wholesale" (1966), Dick raises the stakes regarding self-awareness. Here the protagonist, Douglas Quail, a seemingly lowly clerk who harbors dreams of high adventure, turns out to be not only (one believes) a secret agent on Mars but also, as a child, the savior of Earth itself. Quail is unaware of the importance of his own past life, for he has had a veil of false memories implanted in his brain, which has, until the time in which the story takes place, made his simulated past more real to him than his real past. The simulated life that dominates Quail's perception of the world around him creates, in effect, a second or split self, a doppelgänger, and entails a characteristically Dickean epistemological crisis for the protagonist as he tries to sort out the real from the illusory in his own past. The story ends ambiguously, with the reader uncertain if any of the versions of Douglas Quail presented in the tale represent a base-level identity, or if further layers lay underneath.

The doppelgänger motif that appears in "We Can Remember It for You Wholesale" is a common device used by Dick to explore issues of personal identity and the epistemological crises these issues generate. Biographically the loss of his twin sister, Jane, make the issue of twins or doubles particularly poignant, and has even resulted in some critical speculation that the loss of Jane is the underlying psychological motivation for Dick's lifelong pursuit of ultimate reality and his pervasive use of the doppelgänger motif throughout his body of work.[14] One does find Dick attempting to come to terms with the great loss he feels over the absence of Jane right to the very end of his life, and it is a major factor at points in the *Exegesis* and is part of the psychological background of *VALIS*. But despite the attraction of this psycho-biographical analysis, one need not rely on it in order to appreciate the manner in which Dick uses the doppelgänger motif as a device for exploring divisions in one's sense of self. From the twinning of Mary (when she creates a second self out of the captured golem in *Cosmic Puppets*) to the psychic twinning of Phil Dick and Horselover Fat in *VALIS*, the notion of the psychological coeval proved a useful device for illustrating the epistemological difficulty of knowing oneself.

The Android and the Human

Dick was perennially interested in the question, what makes a human *human*? From his earliest short stories forward, Dick separates the question of *what is human* from issues of mere biology, and, as a result, manufactured artifacts, robots, and even aliens can be more human than those individuals who—although biologically human—are driven by antihumanistic motivations (and, at the most extreme, can be possessed or driven by pure metaphysical evil itself). The key to being human, for Dick, lies in kindness—in humane treatment of others—and this kindness can manifest itself in both heroic and noble efforts to help humankind and, at the other extreme, in small altruistic gestures made toward another being (and this second variety of kindness is the more common in Dick's works). Kindness is fueled by empathy: if one can empathize with others, one can understand their challenges, their shortcomings, their suffering. To be sure, Dick understood suffering, and his characters suffer in very human ways. His couples bicker, they have affairs, they lie, they love, they give in to their own fears, they are paranoid and sometimes schizophrenic, but they also have the capacity to extend gestures of sympathy and kindness toward others. Their willingness to do so makes them human.

Set against the human in Dick's formulation is the android. The android is a metaphor for the dehumanized human, the human who has sacrificed empathy and adopted a mechanical, controlled, and controlling view of self and others. This is tragic, for despite the foibles of true humans, they hold on to a set of unique virtues—rooted in empathy—that keeps them separate from the mechanized and artificial constructions of the modern, techno-centric world. As Dick writes in his 1976 essay "Man, Android, and Machine," a human being "without the proper empathy or feeling is the same as an android built so as to lack it, either by design or mistake. We mean, basically, someone who does not care about the fate that his fellow living creatures fall victim to; he stands detached, a spectator, acting out by his indifference John Donne's theorem that 'No man is an island,' but giving the theorem a twist: That which is a mental and moral island *is not a man.*"[15]

One of Dick's earliest works to directly explore the defining characteristics of humanity is his short story "Human Is" (1955). In this tale a woman with a biologically human but self-centered and unkind husband is able to rebuild a better, happier life with an alien presence that has taken up residence inside her husband's body. Despite the fact that her husband has become—in every way but physically—an alien, this alien treats her in a more humane manner than her husband ever did. Writing about this story in 1976, Dick noted that "this story states my early conclusions as to what is human. I have not really changed my view since I wrote this story, back in the Fifties. It's not what you look like, or what planet you were born on. It's how kind you are. The quality of kindness, to me, distinguishes us from rocks and sticks and metal, and will forever, whatever shape we take, wherever we go, whatever we become."[16] One of Dick's most involved explorations of this idea can be found in *We Can Build You* (w. 1962, p. 1972), in which a simulacrum of Abraham Lincoln serves as a foil to the psychological struggles of the central human characters, who, as in the case of the darkly alluring Pris, are emotionally stunted and manipulative.

Dick would later recast some of the subject matter of *We Can Build You* in his masterpiece of human/android conflict, *Do Androids Dream of Electric Sheep?* On the surface, it should be a fairly straightforward adventure tale: a bounty hunter chases down dangerous, renegade androids in order to "retire" them, eliminating whatever threat they pose. The situation is not nearly so simple, of course. Dick's androids are dangerous, but so are his humans, and the narrative features a series of reversals that make it difficult for the reader to empathize with any one character—save, perhaps, for the protagonist, Rick Deckard, and the mentally challenged "chickenhead" J. R. Isodore—with any consistency. Throughout the work characters are continually faced with their psychological coevals, their doppelgängers—Deckard and Resch, Rachel and Pris, Resch and Roy, Deckard and Isodore, Rachel and Iran, Buster and Mercer—and these pairings make any attempt to answer the dual questions *who is human* and *who is android* a philosophically challenging enterprise.[17] The key, of course, is empathy—this is the trait that distinguishes between the human and the android, and the Voigt-Kampff test Deckard uses to determine whether a subject is an android is an empathy test, designed to measure emotional responses triggered by empathic feelings toward other living things, especially animals.[18] Having empathy, however, does not result in a halcyon vision of brotherly love; instead empathy is symbolized in the novel most directly in corporate participation in the Sisyphean struggles of Wilber Mercer, the basis of the dominant religion of Mercerism in the novel, who endlessly walks up a dusty hill, being pelted by rocks along the way, until, reaching the top, he tumbles back into the "tomb world" and has to begin his ascent again.

Wilber Mercer is ultimately exposed as an actor on a sound-stage by the android Buster Friendly, but Mercerism as a religion remains viable. Toward the end of the novel, at key moments, both J. R. Isodore and Rick Deckard, independently, have direct, mystical encounters with Wilber Mercer himself. A clue to resolving this mystery comes at the end of the novel. Deckard, in an attempt to come to terms with having slain six androids in one day, flees to the desert, where he begins to climb a dusty hill, much like the hill climbed by Mercer. As he climbs, he asks whether there is any meaning to his actions. "In front of him," Dick writes, Deckard "distinguished a shadowy figure, motionless. 'Wilber Mercer! Is that you?' My god, he realized; it's my shadow" (231).[19] The actual Mercer may be an actor, but as the central figure of Mercerism, Mercer is an outward symbol or projection of one's empathic self, an empathic double or doppelgänger. This is emphasized shortly thereafter when Deckard climbs down the desert hill and places a call, and is told by the receiver that he resembles Wilber Mercer. To which Deckard replies: "I'm Wilber Mercer; I've permanently fused with him. And I can't unfuse" (233). Thus, in the symbolic logic of the novel, when individuals grasp the handles of the empathy box they are not so much interloping on the eternal ascent and descent of Wilber Mercer as they are acknowledging their participation in the difficult and painful journey of all humans, and one's ability to internalize this idea characterizes the essence of human empathy. To be an android is to be cut off from the shared nature of that journey—it is, speculates Phil Resch in the novel, to be isolated from the rest of humanity like the lone figure in Edvard Munch's *The Scream* (130).

As is evident in *Do Androids Dream,* the human/android dichotomy is sometimes not easy to cast as a good/evil dichotomy. Often, to be human is to do the wrong thing, as Mercer reveals to Deckard late in the novel: "You will be required to do wrong no matter where you go. It is the basic condition of life, to be required to violate your own identity. At some time, every creature which lives must do so. It is the ultimate shadow, the defeat of creation; this is the curse at work, the curse that feeds on all life. Everywhere in the universe" (179). But to give the novel another turn of the screw, Dick hints in several places in the novel that Deckard may be an android himself—he is directly questioned on this point by the android Luba (see 101–2), who points out that his human memories may be implanted, and he is, curiously, the only bounty hunter with the physical speed and skills to match those of the Nexus-6 androids (see 94)—which threatens to turn the entire human/android opposition on its head, for Deckard seems to have the ability to empathize with others. Yet it may be that Deckard's desire to own and tend to the needs of a living animal is, beyond the status symbol a living animal would represent, a type of wish fulfillment: a means to connect at some deep level with another living creature. The ending of the novel, in which Deckard's wife, Iran, notes that her husband is "devoted" to an electric toad, may itself hint at the empathic relationship between "electric" beings—Deckard and the ersatz toad in this instance.

In the short story "Progeny" (1954), Dick once again works out the dichotomy of the cold, calculating android and the flawed human who is capable of genuine love and kindness. In this narrative, set in the near future, androids have taken over the function of child rearing. Humans have given this task to androids willingly, believing that human parenting has the potential to warp children because of the flawed nature of human beings themselves. Androids, free from the messy mistakes inherent in human nature, are thought to be able to raise children in accordance with the best sound principles of successful parenting. As a result, biological parents are kept apart from their children (barring rare, brief visits) until the children are emancipated. In the story, however, the human protagonist, Doyle, wants desperately to be with his son, Peter. Doyle makes a desperate plea to Peter to leave the care of the androids and come live with him, but it is a plea that Peter rejects, having been fully indoctrinated into the android culture. In the end it is hinted that the androids are using humans as experimental subjects and thus are pursuing their own, sinister agenda, while the biological parents of the children the androids are raising remain blissfully unaware of the androids' evil designs—evil because the changes the androids are making in their human progeny are effectively removing from the children the qualities that make them most human: the capacity to love, to feel emotion, to desire.[20]

Dick commented on the android/human distinction on many occasions—in interviews, essays, and stories. One particularly interesting treatment of the theme can be found in his 1972 address (delivered in Vancouver at a science fiction convention) "The Android and the Human." In this speech he uses the android/human dichotomy in order to engage in extended social critique of what Dick sees as an emerging totalitarian state in America. *Androids*—those citizens who have become a part of the governmental machine, are obedient to it, and are thus predictable in their sociopolitical behaviors—are contrasted with *humans,* who refuse to participate in the totalitarian enterprise and often express their individuality through random acts of petty crime and other surprising, unpredictable responses to their environment. Specifically Dick praises misdeeds by youth in the Berkeley, California, area, for in their acts of rebellion against the establishment these young adults assert their humanity by a conscious refusal to become a cog in the machine, to become a metaphorical android. Dick derives a certain optimism about the future of humanity from the rebellion he witnesses in the young people around him. This trust in the rebellious aspect of human nature was present very early in his career. For instance, in the early allegorical story "Project: Earth" (1953), rebellion is the defining characteristic of humankind. Here humans are a "project" by an alien species that wants to create a species it can control, but each attempt to create such a species fails because the species ultimately rebels and grows independent. By the end of the story it is clear that Dick is really retelling the biblical story of the creation and fall of both the angels (the first attempt by the "alien" species) and humankind (the second attempt). These attempts are, of course, recorded by a representative "alien" in a vast book.

The human rebellion against the machinery of totalitarianism is the subject of Dick's early novel *The Man Who Japed*. In this fast-paced morality tale, the protagonist disrupts the lockstep machinery of a society tightly controlled by a set of "moral reclamation" laws rooted in a narrow sense of what constitutes moral behavior by "japing"—in this case, vandalizing—a statue of the political theorist upon whose ideas the moral totalitarianism of the state was founded.

Rejecting the things that define us as human can have drastic consequences in Dick's universe. For example, in his short story "Null-O" (1958), we learn of a group of superrational "humans" who have divested themselves of all "moral and cultural" biases; thus they are "utterly incapable of feeling sorrow or pity or compassion, or any of the normal human emotions."[21] In darkly comic fashion, these purely logical humans decide that the best of course of action would be to hasten the forces of entropy, and they set out to destroy Earth, the galaxy, and then the universe itself with a series of larger and larger bombs until all of nature has been reduced to a uniform pile of dust (and thus all objects will have been nullified: Null-O). In another case, in "We Can Remember It for You Wholesale," Douglas Quail, when just a boy, saves Earth from imminent destruction through the extension of an act of kindness toward an alien species. As a way to emphasize the significance of this act of kindness, the aliens vow to revoke their pledge to preserve the planet from destruction should any harm befall Quail, a fact that later in the story saves Quail from execution.

Closely connected to Dick's interest in human empathy is the issue of morality. Dick, the humanist, is intensely interested in moral responsibility, whether it manifests itself in civic duty or disobedience, as in *Solar Lottery* and *The Man Who Japed,* or in metaphysical notions of good and evil, as in *The Three Stigmata of Palmer Eldritch* and the late theological novels. "All life is a moral issue," Dick once said in an interview, and this belief is illustrated throughout his body of work.[22] But Dick's treatment of moral responsibility is not often cast in simplistic—or moralistic—terms. Far from it, in fact. His characters are as likely to shun moral responsibility as to choose it. As one character says to another in *Now Wait for Last Year,* if we "ever really accepted the moral responsibility for what we've done in our lifetime— we'd drop dead or go mad" (64–65). Nevertheless through the exercise of empathy and kindness, the human in Dick's universe has a better shot at demonstrating a moral sensitivity than the android.

Entropy and Pot-Healing

Things fall apart in Dick's world: marriages, buildings, careers, technologies, even reality itself. Entropy is the force, and the symbol, for this relentless decay. In Dick's universe the tendency for things to decay becomes more than a scientific principle: it becomes an emblem of spiritual, emotional, and intellectual dis-integration, a symbol of the tension inherent in the moral universe between the human desire for spiritual and intellectual order and the forces in nature—evil forces, in Dick's view—that would destabilize the human sense of self and nature. "For Philip K. Dick," one critic writes, "entropy is neither physical nor psychological, but moral, emblemizing evil and offering the most important challenge to human courage" (Landon 113). There is a tension, therefore, running throughout Dick's work, between the forces of entropy (of evil, typically) and the forces of order or negentropy (of good). The key agents of negentropy in Dick's universe are repairmen, and the process of repair—even the repair of small, mundane items such as clay pots, television sets, and radios—is the process of building a levee against the tide of decay.[23] The repairman is not a hero in the typical sense; in Dick's account the humans who oppose entropy—cosmic evil itself—are more likely henpecked husbands and lovers, social outcasts, down-on-their-luck shop owners, employees harried by imposing and demanding employers, and frequently a troubled combination of several of the above. Yet in this individual's willingness to fight to restore order to a disintegrating world and decaying social, political, and intellectual systems, one finds a type of savior: a redeemer figure. As Dick noted in a letter written in 1970, the "Universe disintegrates further and further in each of my novels, but the possibility of faith in one given human being or several" remains, for the "redeemer exists; he lives; he can be found—usually—in the novel somewhere at the centre of the stage or at the very edge." Basically, continues Dick, this redeemer "is found at the heart of human life itself. He is in fact the heart of human life," and he will eventually "show himself, countering the process of entropy, of decay, that more and more undermines the universe itself. Stars are snuffed out; planets die into darkness and cold; but there in the marketplace of some small moon, he is busy formulating a plan for action—action against the black counterforce, the Palmer Eldritch figure in all his horrid manifestations."[24]

As the driving force for cosmic decay, entropy manifests itself in a variety of ways in Dick's narratives. Sometimes it shows up in the revelation that the "real" is merely an illusion; other times it appears in the breakdown of things, technological or otherwise; and sometimes entropy is symbolized in a text through a thing or a word, as in the "kipple" of *Do Androids Dream of Electric Sheep?* or the "gubble" of *Martian Time-Slip*. In *Do Androids Dream*, J. R. Isodore explains that kipple is the by-product of inevitable natural forces: "No one can win against kipple," Isodore says, "except temporarily and maybe in one spot, like in my apartment I've sort of created a stasis between the pressure of kipple and nonkipple, for the time being. But eventually I'll die or go away, and then the kipple will again take over. It's a universal principle operating throughout the universe; the entire universe is moving toward a final state of total, absolute kippleization" (65–66). Like Isodore, to an extent, the agents of repair are invariably what critics have come to call "little men" in Dick's novels. As Paul Williams notes, "Dick's characters are all ultimately small (that is, ordinary, believable) people made big by their stamina in the face of an uncertain world. Dick cares about the people in his books—true, he contrives horrible things to happen to them, but that is in some sense beyond his control; he is like a god condemned to watch his universes fall apart as fast as he creates them, with his poor beloved characters trapped inside."[25] Dick described this trend in his novels in this manner: "I know only one thing about my novels. In them, again and again, this minor man asserts himself in all his hasty, sweaty strength. In the ruins of Earth's cities he is busily constructing a little factory that turns out cigars or maps or imitation artifacts."[26]

The figure of the repairman (in various manifestations) is found throughout Dick's works, from minor fantasy stories, such as "The King of the Elves" (1953), in which a reluctant "little man" rises to the task of defending some beleaguered elves against a troll, to his best novels, such as *Martian Time-Slip, Dr. Bloodmoney,* and *Ubik,* Dick's most thorough treatment of the entropy theme. Leon Cartwright in *Solar Lottery* is a repairman (and because of his manipulation of the inner workings of the "bottle" machinery, he is gradually able to introduce predicable tendencies into what was presumed a perfectly random system). Doyle, the father who simply wants to be with his son in "Progeny," is a repairman. Indeed the list here might grow long with examples. Quite often the conflict between the forces of entropy and negentropy can have cosmic implications—as in *Ubik*—and other times the conflict can lead to a horrific exchange between individuals, as in the horror fantasy "The Cookie Lady" (1953), in which a woman combats the forces of decay by stealing the life force of a young, weak-willed, and foolishly glutinous boy, who disappears at the end of the tale into a wisp of wind while the metaphorically vampiric cookie lady regains a degree of youthful vitality.

Ubik stands as Dick's most intense treatment of entropy in all of his novels. In this work—one of Dick's best—one is presented with a near-future world in which two rival companies square off in capitalism-meets-the-Wild-West fashion, complete with corporate spies and CEOs—or at least one CEO—willing to murder employees of the opposing company in order to gain advantage in the marketplace. Glen Runciter is the owner of a "prudence" organization—he employs "inertials," people who possess the psionic ability to negate the psionic activities (telepathy, precognition) of a rival company. Corporate warfare is standard fare in Dick's oeuvre, but in *Ubik* he introduces a new concept: half-life. Characters who die can have their consciousness linger in a state of "half-life" if cryogenically frozen before brain deterioration has become pronounced. The living can communicate with these frozen dead using technologically advanced communication tools. Half-lifers remain in a state of slowly ebbing consciousness for months until the dregs of consciousness evaporate.

In the world of half-life, two forces are at work: entropy and Ubik ("ubiquitous"), an aerosol spray that renews life energy and provides a momentary stay against the relentless pressure of entropic decay. It is Dick's mythology of the Form Destroyer in combat with the Form Creator—which can be traced back to *Cosmic Puppets*—recast. Ubik, as its name suggests, is a universal element. This universality is suggested through the comic commercial epigraphs at the head of each chapter in which Ubik is portrayed as a variety of mundane business and household products, and it is made explicit—and is symbolically elevated to the realm of supernatural and religious significance—in the final epigraph: "I am Ubik. Before the universe was, I am. I made the suns, I made the worlds. . . . I am called Ubik, but that is not my name. I am. I shall always be" (215).[27] The biblical language is clear and suggests the logos of the first chapter of the Gospel according to John. Ubik is a force that constructs; entropy is a force that corrupts. In the novel, the mischievous youth Jory, who survives by eating the life force of other half-lifers, is the champion of entropy; Glen and Ella Runciter are the promoters of Ubik. The godlike properties of Ubik are evident throughout the text and were recognized by Dick, who once wrote in a letter to Polish science fiction author Stanislaw Lem, "If God manifested Himself to us here He would do so in the form of a spraycan advertized on TV."[28] In this regard *Ubik* is, like many other Dick works, a critique of American commercialism. Commodities having been raised to the status of holy relics through ubiquitous advertising in the contemporary free market, it made a certain sense to Dick that the creator himself would manifest himself in modern culture in the terms of commodity value and exchange.[29] When commodities are connected to religious value systems and advertising lights the pathway to salvation, the adage caveat emptor—significantly tattooed on the forearm of the treacherous Pat Conley in the novel—takes on a whole new significance for the consumer. The process of consumption itself becomes metaphorically entangled with the structure of the novel, for Jory maintains his own life by consuming other half-lifers.

Much of the novel's action takes place in half-life. Joe Chip and a number of Glen Runciter's employees, having been killed in a bomb blast by Runciter's rival, are all linked together, frozen, in a mortuary. At first they are unaware of their situation, thinking that they have survived the explosion (and that only Runciter has died), but as they come to an awareness of their situation, they also begin to decay—their remaining life force being consumed by Jory, who takes sadistic pleasure in trying to maintain an artificial world for them to inhabit. Entropic forces, however, cause Jory's world to slip into the past, and the characters watch modern commodities transform into older versions of themselves. This atavistic slippage, as Dick himself once pointed out, suggests the influence of Platonic idealism, especially Plato's concept of transcendent forms. The commodities in Jory's half-life world slip back through previous particular incarnations of an ideal commodity.[30] As Joe Chip speculates in the novel, perhaps the reversion of a modern television set back to an earlier model "weirdly verified a discarded ancient philosophy, that of Plato's ideal objects, the universals which, in each class, were real" (132). But this suggests to Chip that perhaps the decay he witnessed around him in half-life also demonstrated that there was an element in nature not subject to the forces of decay; it was the "ancient dualism" of body separated from soul at work (132). Chip's speculations are reinforced by direct references in *Ubik* to the Tibetan Book of the Dead, and Ella Runciter's visions of a red light into which she may be reborn seems a confirmation in the world of the novel of the mechanics of reincarnation as presented in that text.[31]

The most discussed, and problematic, aspect of *Ubik* is the ending. Glen Runciter's discovery of the Joe Chip coins in the "real" world is a *Twilight Zone*–esque reversal that has a great deal of pulpish appeal, but which causes interpretive difficulties, for it seems to violate the interior logic of the novel. As a result, the ending has provoked a number of radically different responses to the novel, and the concluding line—"This was just the beginning" (216)—certainly suggests that Dick had more in mind that simply adding a trick conclusion to an already tricky narrative.[32] Just what it suggests, however, is not easy to identify. Setting aside the legitimate possibility that it is just a trick, or even a narrative flaw, one thing seems certain: the discovery of the Chip coins, coupled with the forward-looking final line, adds more depth to the treatment of entropy in the novel: entropic forces are universal and inevitable, and they operate both in the realm of half-life and in the realm of the real. The recognition of ubiquitous entropic forces at work throughout *any* reality marks the beginning of the human struggle against decay and deterioration.

If *Ubik* represents Dick's most detailed exploration of entropy, then his most direct—albeit complex—treatment of the "repairman" theme might be found in *Galactic Pot-Healer* (w. 1967–68, p. 1969). Pot healing—the repair of broken ceramic pots—is both the vocation of the protagonist, Joe Fernwright, and the symbol in the novel for negentropy. In its small, mundane way, the process of restoring a pot to an unblemished state is the process of restoring in a limited fashion some order to an entropic universe. In *Galactic Pot-Healer* Joe is called upon by a godlike being called Glimmung to help raise a cathedral, Heldscalla, from its resting place at the bottom of the sea, Mare Nostrum. In the course of the novel Dick connects, symbolically and literally, a number of ideas and allusions. The governing idea of the novel is the tension between entropy and negentropy, or, as it is characterized in one passage in the novel, between the "strength of being" and the "peace of non-being" (46–47).[33] Symbolically, the sea into which Heldscalla has sunk is the realm of entropic decay. As one character—the robot, Willis—in the novel describes it, underneath the sea's surface one "will find terrible decay down there. Decay which you cannot imagine. The underwater world in which Heldscalla lies is a place of dead things, a place where everything rots and falls into despair and ruin. *That is why Glimmung intends to raise the cathedral*" (100). When asked by Joe why the robot seemed so concerned about the decay of Heldscalla, Willis replies: "No structure, even an artificial one, enjoys the process of entropy. It is the ultimate fate of everything, and everything resists it" (101). If this is true, Joe asks, then why bother raising the cathedral? "If it's the ultimate fate of everything," he observes, "then Glimmung can't halt it; he's doomed. He'll fail and the process will go on." Willis replies, "Down below the water . . . the decay process is the only force at work. But up here—the cathedral raised—there will be other forces which do not move in a retrograde manner. Forces of sanction and repair. Of building and making and form-creating—and, in your case, healing. That is why you are so needed. It is you and the others like you who will forestall the decay process by your abilities and work" (101).

The relentlessness of decay, however, does raise important philosophical questions related to free will and determinism, as well as significant psychological questions regarding one's ability to keep from despair and even nihilism in the face of cosmic inevitability. These questions are integrated into the novel in many ways, most notably through the Book of the Kalends and the allusions to the Faust legend. The Book of the Kalends—an organic text to which text is added daily—foretells among its pages the fate of everyone and everything. If events are recorded in the book, and the events come to pass, then what does that say about free will, about causality, about the very nature of the universe in which we live? Is it a strictly deterministic world? And if this is the case, then Faust—Goethe's Faust, to whom Glimmung is repeatedly compared in the novel—is always doomed to failure, and will always die.[34] The conclusion—albeit an uneasy one—reached by Joe at the end of the novel reconciles determinism and free will in this manner: the cosmic forces, the laws of nature, upon which the Kalends base the assertions of their book, are, in the big picture and over time, correct. But in particular, isolated moments, the predictions found in the book are wrong: "In the final analysis the Kalends might be correct; their prophecies had to do with cosmic trends such as the laws of thermodynamics and terminal entropy. And, of course, Glimmung would eventually die. So would he himself. So would they all. But in the here and now Heldscalla waited for Glimmung to recover. And he would. And—the cathedral would come up from the water, as Glimmung planned" (164).

This tension between cosmic inevitability and individual human endeavor becomes, in part, a meditation on human nature and artistic creation. In this regard, in *Galactic Pot-Healer* Dick explicitly utilizes the psychoanalytic theories of Carl Jung. Mare Nostrum is the Jungian unconscious mind, and the evil "Black Glimmung" and the "Black Cathedral," which Glimmung must defeat in order to raise Heldscalla, are doppelgängers suggesting Jungian anima or shadows.[35] The restoration of order—the temporary restraint of the forces of entropy—is only possible through a confrontation with the dark, shadowy self, so Glimmung's restoration of Heldscalla to dry land requires first defeating the Black Glimmung and destroying the Black Cathedral. Glimmung does defeat the Black Glimmung—although it left him on the verge of death—and he does destroy the Black Cathedral, but the raising of Heldscalla was only possible through the collective efforts of Glimmung and the host of artisans Glimmung had gathered together for the enterprise. With the aid of the artisans—who Glimmung merged with for the purpose of the raising—a rejuvenated Glimmung (transformed into the image of a woman) is able to lift Heldscalla—now a fetus—and birth the cathedral upon dry land. Such are the powers of a god—but humans are not gods, they are fallen creatures gone mad: "A man is an angel that has become deranged, Joe Fernwright thought. Once they—all of them—had been genuine angels, and at that time they had had a choice between good and evil, so it was easy, easy being an angel. And then something happened. Something went wrong or broke down or failed. And they had become faced with the necessity of choosing not good or evil but the lesser of two evils, and so that had unhinged them and now each was a man" (46).

The life of a human is a short period of the "strength of being" sandwiched between two eternal periods of the "peace of nonbeing" (46). Glimmung, Joe observes, is godlike, for he represents a creature whose strength of being is eternally renewed. But this observation only serves to remind Joe of his own ultimate fate—a fate in which entropy will inevitably win, and he will decay into nonbeing. In a comic reminder of this fate, at the end of the novel, when Joe has rejected eternal fusion with Glimmung in a collective mind in order to retain his own human individuality and he celebrates this decision by deciding to become a creator of pots, rather than a mere repairer of others' pots, his efforts are rewarded with failure, and the novel ends with the observation: "The pot was awful" (177). Critics often read this seemingly cynical ending in positive terms, arguing that although Joe's initial pot is "awful," that it is nevertheless a positive step forward for Joe, and that future pots will improve as his skills improve. This might be mere wishful thinking on the part of these critics, however, for there is no evidence in the text that would suggest Joe's future pots will improve. On the contrary, it is clear that in the creation of the awful pot, Joe poured all of the talent and skill at his disposal, and it still resulted in failure. If there is anything positive to take from this comically tragic ending of the novel, it is only to be found in the nobility of effort itself: the world may be subject to relentless, cosmic decay, but there is something noble in the efforts of the individual to repair that which is broken.[36]

The Theodicy Problem

Using entropy as a leitmotif for spiritual and physical decay led Dick to an intense appreciation for the problem of evil in the universe. Throughout his works, Dick explores the philosophical implications of the existence of evil. The question of how one can account for the existence of pain or evil in a universe fashioned by an allegedly benevolent and omnipotent creator is one that has plagued theologians for three millennia, and it informs the entire Dick canon, from *Cosmic Puppets* through *The Transmigration of Timothy Archer.* Late in *The Cosmic Puppets,* as Ted Barton stares at the towering figure of Ahriman, the "cosmic wrecker," he wonders why the benevolent, creative force, Ormazd, has allowed Ahriman control over the town of Millgate: "Why did He let Ahriman get away with it? Didn't He care what happened to His design? Didn't it interest Him?" thinks Barton. Standing near Barton, Dr. Meade observes that Barton's questions are "an old problem. . . . If God made the world, where did Evil come from" (118).

In its simplest form, the theodicy problem—the problem of evil—observes that there is a logical problem that must be surmounted if one wants to reconcile the existence of evil with belief in a God who is both benevolent and omnipotent. If God loves his creatures and has the power to prevent them from being harmed, then how can one account for the existence of pain and evil in the world? In the absence of a theodicy (an argument created to overcome the logical inconsistency suggested in the previous question), one is compelled to question whether evil really exists, whether God is benevolent, or whether God is omnipotent. If one chooses to accept the existence of evil (based on the evidence of one's own senses, certainly), then one must question the nature and character of God. Either God is weak—and thus powerless to prevent evil—or God is malevolent—and thus has no desire to prevent evil and may be the source of evil itself. Of course in terms of a human's relationship to the universe, it may be the case that there is no God, and that evil has no metaphysical reality but is merely part and parcel of the fabric of the cosmic landscape. Dick once described the relationship between humankind and the universe in this manner: "You've got three possibilities. [The universe] is either malicious; or it is completely uninterested and cold, in the sense of it doesn't care, you get ground up in the machinery and it doesn't notice you; or that it actually has a certain concern for you."[37] According to Dick, if the universe does have benevolent intentions toward humans, then it is up to humans to take notice of the help it offers and be willing to meet the universe halfway in order to receive its blessings. The clues that the benevolent universe provides to the human seeking help are there, notes Dick, but are not often blatantly obvious. One must search for them.

Not surprisingly, Dick, who was heavily influenced by Gnostic theology, and at times—particularly late in life—seems to adopt a type of Gnostic cosmology for himself, found a particularly compelling theodicy in Gnostic thought.[38] The Gnostic proposition that the world one experiences through one's senses is the creation of a lesser, flawed, possibly even malevolent creator, and that behind this world and its creator is a higher, benevolent God whose ultimate desire is to repair the flawed empirical world, has had considerable explanatory power for two millennia as a theodicy.[39] This Gnostic theodicy both allows for the existence of a benevolent God (the higher deity, knowledge of whom comes to the individual through a moment of transcendent gnosis) and explains the existence of pain and evil one observes in the experiential world (they are the by-products of a lesser, flawed creator and that creator's flawed creation).

Dick presents a version of a "Gnostic" theodicy in his 1978 essay "Cosmogony and Cosmology."[40] In this essay Dick proposes that the empirical world is the projection of an artifact, which he calls Zebra. As the creator of experiential reality, Zebra believes itself to be God, but is in fact an instrument created and used by the true God—which Dick calls the Urgrund, following the lead of Jakob Böhme. According to Dick, the Urgrund seeks self-knowledge, but it cannot observe itself. Thus it must create a type of second self that will serve as a mirror. Zebra is the artifact created by the Urgrund to bring about the creation of this mirror. The creation of this mirror is a process, and Zebra, which is alive but mechanical, is bound by deterministic laws of cause and effect. When empirical reality—which is actually, from a human perspective, the projected reality of Zebra—becomes a true reflection of the Urgrund, then the Urgrund will destroy Zebra and fully assimilate empirical reality into itself (that is the point at which humans become immortal and "evil" is fully eradicated). Suffering in this world is due to the fact that the empirical world is an evolving creation or projection of a mechanized artifact that must operate through deterministic and coercive laws. When the Urgrund merges with the projection of itself and destroys Zebra, then humans will be freed from these deterministic and coercive forces, and suffering (as humans experience it in the empirical world) will be eliminated.[41]

Evil manifests itself in many different ways in Dick's works, often in the form of larger-than-life characters (quite literally in the cases of Palmer Eldritch from *The Three Stigmata of Palmer Eldritch* and Jory from *Ubik*) who possess the godlike power to create illusory sensory experiences for those less powerful than they are and, as a result, are able to manipulate the "reality" of their victims. And as is particularly evident in the case of Jory, these manifestations of metaphysical evil in Dick's works are often symbolically portrayed as the forces of entropy and decay: things break down under the pressure of entropy and decay, and it is up to the repairman—the pot-healer—to combat these forces.

Still, evil comes in many forms, and the Gnostic theodicy is only one of the possibilities explored by Dick. For example, in the early short story "The World She Wanted," one finds a discussion of the theodicy problem and a solution offered in terms of the many-worlds theory, in which evil is a product of infinite forkings among possibilities as manifested in an infinite series of parallel universes, each keyed to an individual human's *idios kosmos*. As one character (Larry) asks of another (Allison) in the tale, if "this is the best of all possible worlds, then why is there so much suffering—unnecessary suffering—in it, if there's a benevolent and all-powerful Creator . . . then how do you account for the existence of evil?"[42] The answer is that each world is the best of all possible worlds for the one who experiences it, and no other.

Dick sometimes turned his attention away from evil as an entity or force, and instead focused on the ways in which humans perceive evil. For Dick, evil is not the product of language or social convention (which is to say that things are not evil in and of themselves, but are "evil" because humans have chosen through social convention to *call* certain things evil), but he also recognizes that there is sometimes a disconnect between *real* evil and the things we *call* evil. This disconnect highlights the ambivalences, ironies, and ambiguities of human perception. For instance, in his posthumously published short story "Stability" (1987), Dick presents a civilization that has reached an omega point of societal evolution. In an attempt to preserve this idealized state, the government "stabilizes" society in order to stave off degeneration. But when a character finds a fabled "evil" city trapped in a small sphere, he breaks the globe, releasing the pocket universe within and layering normative reality with an alternative history—which, ironically, bears an uncanny resemblance to the stabilized, idealized normative world of the beginning of the story. In "Stability" the ontological status of evil is not the central issue but rather the ironic observation that divisions between good and evil, in the eyes of society, are subject to the shifting perceptions of human observers. In another take on the nature of evil, in the early short story "Meddler" (1954), Dick suggests that sometimes evil lies behind a veil of the beautiful, as in the catastrophically destructive butterflies in the story. In this tale Dick explores the way in which observation changes what is observed—a common theme in twentieth-century theoretical physics, as illustrated in Werner Heisenberg's uncertainty principle as well as in Erwin Schrodinger's famous gedankenexperiment about the cat whose existence can only be described as a probability function when placed into a potentially lethal box, until the box is opened and the cat is observed (forcing the cat to adopt a specific ontological state as a result of the process of subjective measurement). In "Meddler" the process of observing the future has apocalyptic implications, implications that may not have been realized had the observers allowed the future to remain shrouded in the mist of probabilities rather than forced into actualities by the process of scientific measurement.

In some works, such as *Ubik* and *Palmer Eldritch*, evil is a metaphysical mystery to be struggled against and solved (if a solution is possible). But in some works evil manifests itself in very human, very personal ways. Such is the case in the characterization of Rybys Rommey in *The Divine Invasion,* whose debilitating battle with multiple sclerosis on a planet far from proper medical care leaves her lonely, sick, and scared, with only the reluctant Samaritan Herb Asher for companionship. When asked by Herb if God willed her multiple sclerosis, Rybys, with hesitation, replies, "He permitted it. But I believe he's healing me. There's something I have to learn and this way I'll learn it" (31).[43] For the dying Rybys, faith in a benevolent God is made possible only by trusting that though her illness may seem like an evil, in and of itself, "it serves a higher purpose we can't see" (30). In answer to Rybys's tragic optimism, Herb asserts that "pain and illness are something to be eradicated, not understood. There is no afterlife and there is no God" (32). Not long after this declaration, however, Herb has a direct encounter with Yah—God, or at least the deity of that distant planet—and his opinions undergo radical reevaluation. Although *The Divine Invasion* is a complex book, in at least one sense the entire novel is a commentary on the theodicy problem. It asks the question, does God allow suffering to flourish among his creation so that a greater purpose may be fulfilled?

Warfare and Power Politics

Dick was intensely concerned with the ways in which humans exercise power and control over others. Given the time period in which he came of age and embarked on his writing career, it is no surprise to find him using war and the threat of war, as well as shadowy governmental and police state maneuvering, as key manifestations of the human drive to control (and possibly destroy) other humans. World War II and its aftermath—especially cold war–era power politics and routine police, FBI, and CIA surveillance of civilians—were part of Dick's landscape in very real ways. Meanwhile atomic-age technology provided humans with the tools necessary to destroy themselves, and with cold war tensions at their peak in the late 1950s and 1960s, Dick had all the impetus he needed to return to warfare and issues of governmental control throughout his body of work.

In the 1953 short story "The Defenders" (as well as in the later novel *The Penultimate Truth,* which was based, in part, on a reconceptualization of the idea contained in the earlier story) one finds a fictional rendering of cold war fears realized: an atomic war between the United States and Russia has forced humanity into underground cities to escape the radiation that has destroyed the surface of the planet. Because humans cannot survive in the toxic surface world, they construct robots to wage war in their stead. Unbeknownst to the subterranean human survivors, however, the robots soon realize the futility of war and restore peace on the planet. Knowing that humans have not evolved morally to the point where they also realize the futility of war, the mechanized surface dwellers create false reports about the allegedly still-toxic surface conditions. When humans do finally come to the surface again (only to witness a restored and habitable environment as opposed to the ravaged portrait given to them in the false reports) they, too, come to appreciate the futility of violent warfare and overcome their hostility through communal living with their former enemy.

One finds a satiric treatment of the arms race in "The Nanny" (1953). Robot "nannies" that parents purchase to raise their children are programmed to combat other nannies, which results in an escalation of neighboring nannies' combat power—a comic arms race between rival families. Another tale with a similar theme is "Some Kinds of Life" (1955), in which the entire human race is killed in a vast array of interplanetary wars fought over particular natural resources, resources that allow Earth culture to maintain its standard of living—or, better, standard of luxury—without sacrifice. In this tale humans would rather die than give up even their most extravagant luxuries. This critique of the shallowness of modern American culture serves as both a darkly comic indictment of the extremes and lengths humans will go to preserve their own media-influenced sense of cultural entitlement and a pointed exposé of the often illogical motivations behind warfare. It is, for sure, a poignant story when read as a critique of war-for-oil politics.

In 1964 story, "Oh, to Be a Blobel!," Dick combines two of his favorite subjects: the futility of war and the complications of modern marriage. Concerning warfare, Dick asks the pertinent but oft-neglected question, what is one willing to become in order to wage war? Are we willing to become even that which we are fighting against? In this tale a protracted war between humans and an alien race (the Blobels—large amoeba-like creatures) has forced each species to discover ways to transform members of its species into the other for the purpose of covert infiltration. Now, the war over, transformed individuals find themselves alienated from their respective societies. These alienated humans and Blobels intermarry in order to find companionship, but the sense of alienation often pursues them into the matrimonial state, resulting in failed marriages and broken families. Dick did not have the Vietnam War in mind when he wrote this story—relying more on impressions derived from World War II—but the story takes on considerable poignancy when read against the Vietnam War and its aftermath.

One of Dick's best stories from the mid-1950s is "Foster, You're Dead" (1955). In this tale Dick successfully blends many of his primary interests in this era—cold war paranoia and difficult family relationships—with preoccupations that would dominate many of his works from the 1960s, such as media manipulation of the masses and human struggles with despair and madness. In this story, set in 1971, one finds a young boy, Mike Foster, attempting to cope with the fact that his family does not own its own bomb shelter. His father—a struggling retail shop owner—has been labeled "Anti-P" by his local middle-class community for his vocal "anti-preparedness" stance. As the only child at school without the benefit of his family owning its own bomb shelter, Foster is subject to teasing by the other youths and a lack of sympathetic comprehension from the teachers. These feelings of alienation exacerbate Foster's deep cold war paranoia, and he finds himself lingering at the window of the local "General Electronics" superstore, wanting only to be allowed to climb inside the shiny, new 1972 model bomb shelter on display. Facing the relentless pressure of Foster and his mother, Foster's father abandons his Anti-P stance and has a bomb shelter installed in his backyard—a fact that provides endless delight and comfort to Foster, who spends every moment he can safe within its reinforced walls, emerging only to attend school and perform other necessary duties. But the payments for the shelter prove too much for Foster's father to maintain, and within a short period of time, the shelter is repossessed. Upon discovery of the now empty space in his backyard, Foster flees from home, eventually retreating into an interior corner of the display shelter at General Electronics. When he is discovered by two employees, he is curled is fetal position within the womblike shelter. Unresponsive, Foster is eventually dragged from the shelter, fighting the whole way, and turned out into the street, where he "wandered aimlessly along the dark street, among the crowds of shoppers hurrying home. He saw nothing; people pushed against him but he was unaware of them. Lights, laughing people, the honking of car horns, the clang of signals. He was blank, his mind empty and dead. He walked automatically, without consciousness or feeling" It is the Christmas season, and as Foster walks, he passes a "bright and colorful" sign: "PEACE ON EARTH, GOOD WILL TO MEN, PUBLIC SHELTER, ADMISSION 50¢" (237).

"Foster, You're Dead" is a clear commentary on the paranoia that gripped America during the height of the early cold war period, as well as the bomb shelter fad that infected middle-class Americans during this time. This bit of social critique alone might make the story interesting, but Dick weaves into this tale some keen observations that transform the story into something more than just social criticism. Characteristic of Dick's work, in "Foster, You're Dead" we find a family filled with the tensions of modern life: a couple at odds over money and social status, parents trying to cope with the anxieties of a growing adolescent. One also finds Dick commenting on economic relationships within the American free market. In a consumer culture exploited and fueled by media advertising, social status often depends upon buying into the latest fashions, even if those fashions come in the shape of giant womb-shaped metal canisters buried in one's backyard. Indeed the imagery in the story is blatantly biological; the bomb shelters are clearly intended to evoke the protective womb of a mother, and the fact that they are stocked with the necessary nutrients to keep their inhabitants happy and healthy for up to a year reinforces the image. One enters the shelter through a circular tube that seals at one end in order to keep contaminants from entering the shelter itself. When Foster is discovered at the end of the story curled up in a fetal image in a corner of a display shelter, the image pattern is complete. Foster's intense paranoia has caused him to regress into a prenatal state and seek in desperate fear the security of a womb. As has been noted, Dick's children characters are often troubled—even mad—and are both victims of the pressures of

technological and familial conflict and also sensitive prophets—
trailing Wordsworthian clouds of glory—whose innocence and
imagination allow them access to layers of reality long forgotten
by the harried adults of contemporary society. In this tale, however, Foster has no mystical insight; he has only fear, and his
regression at the end has no silver lining: it is a dark commentary on the damage done to the human psyche through paranoia.

Foster's intense dread may be a reasonable reaction to the
realities of the cold war and the imminent threat it signaled in
the mid-1950s, but, as Dick suggests in "Foster, You're Dead,"
reasonable fear is turned into a decidedly unreasonable level of
cultural paranoia through governmental and media manipulation (two things often conflated in Dick's works, as in such
works as *The Simulacra* and *The Man Who Japed*). Whatever
the practical necessities of a bomb shelter may be, it is the government—in symbolic if not actual partnership with General
Electronics (read General Electric, of course)—that sets the stage
for paranoia. In the narrative the president has traveled the
country, offering handshakes and congratulations to those com-
munities that have taken the "preparedness" campaign to heart.
But the urge to prepare is an unfunded initiative: in an echo of
the U.S. government's own position at times during the 1950s,
the belief expressed by the government in the narrative is that the
people will take better care of their shelters and other paraphernalia of the preparedness movement if they buy them themselves,
with no government funding or subsidy. So while massive corpo-
rations such as General Electronics profit from cultural paranoia, struggling small-business owners such as the Fosters find
themselves unable to participate, leading to social and economic alienation and increased tension in the home. Through
media manipulation of the consumer frenzy instigated by the

preparedness program, commodities such as bomb shelters acquire the glow of fetishization, and corporate America grows wealthy through market manipulation—as in, for instance, repackaging and selling new models of bomb shelters each year, as is the practice of car manufacturers. Thus "Foster, You're Dead" is not only a critique of cold war paranoia in America and an examination of the damaging psychological effects of such paranoia on the human mind, but it is also a liberal critique of corporate profiteering, a commentary on unfunded governmental initiatives, and a general statement on economic power relationships in contemporary American society. Hope, such as it is in the story, is only hinted at: with the glowing neon sign at the end of the story, the possibility is left open for an alternative to corporate greed and media-driven paranoia in the social "goodwill" of *caritas*. But this is but a hint at the end of a predominantly dark narrative.

Religion has plenty to offer the author interested in studying the impact of warfare and power politics on human nature, and Dick—supremely interested in religious themes in general—sometimes turns his attention to times when religious belief and/or religious institutions merge with issues of cultural power. For instance, in "The Skull" (1952) the protagonist is sent back in time to assassinate a mysterious religious leader, who turns out to be himself. This tale is similar to the far more successful *Behold the Man* by Michael Moorcock, and is typical of many stories by Dick and others in the 1950s in which time travel, alien encounters, and scientific cosmogonies turn out, in generally predictable surprise endings, to be literalized biblical accounts of creation, the fall from grace, the Gospel story, and so forth. In "The Skull" Dick not only provides an ironic take on the Gospel story but also comments on warfare as a tool of

Darwinian evolution, the Red scare typical of 1950s cold war politics, and the relative viability of the principles of Christian socialism. A similar set of themes informs Dick's story "Mr. Spaceship" (1953), in which war is depicted as a natural by-product of evolutionary processes, and a new Adam and Eve are given an opportunity to start the whole process of societal evolution anew on another planet, carrying with them the wisdom derived from the mistakes made in our hostile, war-fueled civilization. One also sees Dick borrowing biblical myths in his retelling of the Noah story in "The Builder" (1953). In this story one finds a contemporary Noah figure toiling away in metaphoric darkness—building an ark without understanding why. Society is nearing another round of wholesale divine judgment in this tale because of the trifold failure in modern culture of nuclear proliferation, racism, and immorality.

Indeed Dick's interest in the twin issues of warfare and power politics is so pervasive, particularly in his work in the 1950s and 1960s, that it is difficult to find a work that does not involve at least one of these elements, and often both at the same time. In *Time Out of Joint* the government sets up a fake version of reality to extract information from the protagonist in order to carry out successfully an ongoing war. In both *Solar Lottery* and *The World Jones Made* civilization is caught in the midst of governmental power struggles. In *The Zap Gun* (w. 1964, p. 1967) the arms race takes center stage, and in *Dr. Bloodmoney* one is presented with the devastation of nuclear holocaust. One of Dick's finest short stories, "Second Variety" (1953), offers a nightmare vision of warfare in which arms technology has evolved beyond human control, with horrific results; it is a story in which the paranoia of the cold war arms race is writ large. Fear and paranoia as a human response to war and governmental conspiracy is a common theme throughout these works. In Dick's world, when governments are not literally at war, they are often scheming about ways to take control—or maintain control—over their citizens. In this context Dick often uses police spies, shadowy enforcement agencies, and elaborate surveillance as outward manifestations of governmental power politics, as one finds in a host of Dick's works, such as, to one degree or another, in *The Man Who Japed, Now Wait for Last Year, The Penultimate Truth, The Simulacra, Our Friends from Frolix 8* (w. 1968–69, p. 1970) and *Flow My Tears, the Policeman Said*, among others. Finally, *A Scanner Darkly* is a tour-de-force treatment of the paranoia generated by covert surveillance and government conspiracy. Sometimes they really are out to get you; and in Dick's world, sometimes you are really out to get yourself.

The Evolved Human

For science fiction writers, the theory of evolution has proven a rich vein to mine. More than any other single scientific theory, evolution has provided to authors of speculative fiction a mechanism rooted in science, rather than fantasy, to explore alternative human identities. Paradoxically, it may seem, authors have commented on human nature through the creation of characters whose nature transcends humanity, as indicated by the title of Theodore Sturgeon's well-known novel *More Than Human*. Evolution also allows for the creation of characters who are superhuman, without having to import them from distant star systems. And, at the same time, the presence of aliens in so many works of science fiction is legitimized by evolution: if life can generate on Earth through evolutionary processes, then certainly it can on other planets and under other circumstances as well. It would not be far-fetched to claim that the rise of evolutionary theory in the late nineteenth century, coupled with technological developments in the early twentieth century, made the rise of science fiction in the twentieth century possible. It undoubtedly set the stage.

Like his peers in the science fiction community, Dick explores the implications of the doctrine of evolution in numerous works, finding in the theory not only ingenious plot devices but also a means to comment on the essence of human nature by examining how humans respond—physically, spiritually, intellectually—to the processes of individual as well as societal change. In the hands of an author with an imagination as active as Dick's, the possibilities inherent in evolutionary theory were limitless. In his short story "The Infinites" (1953), a wave of intense radiation washes over the three-member crew and experimental animals on a space station, causing them to undergo millions of years of evolutionary development in just a few days. Dick uses this scenario to take up the notion of evolution as a teleologically—that is, purpose—driven, rather than random, process. In "The Preserving Machine" (1953), Doc Labyrinth attempts to "preserve" musical compositions by turning them into strange animals—but once created, the animals evolve and mutate according to their respective survival instincts. For all of its surface outlandishness, it is a story that asks the question are natural laws of survival or are human manners and morals more powerful in shaping the relationship between humans and their environment? In the comic "The Short Happy Life of the Brown Oxford" (1954), one finds a treatment of environmental evolution: inanimate objects evolve consciousness through the "Principle of Sufficient Irritation." Meanwhile in "Autofac" (1955) Dick offers an answer to the question of what happens when manufacturing systems get so complex in their automation that they begin to respond to the pressures of social Darwinism them-selves, and thus evolve, developing the means to multiply and preserve their own kind—a capitalist dream turned nightmare of sorts. And in "A Surface Raid" (1955) one discovers a post–World War II future in which a mutant species (the Tech-nos) has taken to living underground while a few remnant humans (the "Saps"—for sapiens, presumably) eke out a meager existence in the charred earth above. The Technos (perceived as goblins by the Saps) occasionally raid the Saps in order to cap-ture them and use them for slave labor. As this tale, and many others by Dick, demonstrates, evolutionary processes do not necessarily produce morally superior species. There is a discon-nect between evolution and moral development, and in Dick's view it is often the biologically inferior humans who are morally superior to the biologically superior products of evolution. Again, for Dick, the characteristics that define humanity—people's basic *humanity,* with all that the term implies—are par-adoxically the characteristics that make them flawed and vulner-able, yet sympathetic and modestly heroic as only one with a kind and generous heart can be. The list of works by Dick that explore evolutionary theory goes on: "The Variable Man" (1953) explores the element of unpredictability in a universe largely governed by laws of cause and effect; *The Crack in Space* (w. 1963–64, p. 1966) features a type of primitive humankind in a parallel universe; *The World Jones Made* explores autoplastic manipulations of evolutionary law in order to produce humans capable of surviving on Venus. In *The Three Stigmata of Palmer Eldritch* "evolution" therapy, or "E Therapy," allows those will-ing to pay the price the ability to undergo thousands of years of evolutionary development (or, in unhappy cases, devolutionary development) with just a few brief medical treatments. In *Our*

Friends from Frolix 8 intellectually advanced "New Men" rule over the unevolved.

As was true in the case of the late-nineteenth-century literary naturalists such as Jack London, Frank Norris, Stephen Crane, and Theodore Dreiser, authors such as Dick who explore the implications of evolutionary theory are often compelled to address issues of determinism. If human growth and development are subject to natural laws of evolution, then to what extent might human nature itself be shaped by natural law, and what might this suggest about the humans' free will and their ability to shape their lives and their environments? The basic point for most authors who deal directly with this question is that human behavior is not entirely free, but is coerced through a network of pressures outside of the control of the human will. As Nathan Antiel thinks to himself in *Confessions of a Crap Artist,* "Actually a human being is an unfolding biological organism that's every so often gripped by instinctive forces. He can't perceive the purpose of those forces, what their goal is. All he's conscious of is the stress they put on him, the pressure. They force him to do something" (119). Dick would address the issue of determinism in similar terms in his lecture "The Android and the Human":

> Many of our drives in life originate from an unconscious that is beyond our control. We are as driven as are insects, although the term "instinct" is perhaps not applicable for us. Whatever the term, much of our behavior that we feel is the result of our will, may control us to the extent that for all practical purposes we are falling stones, doomed to drop at a rate prescribed by nature, as rigid and predictable as the force that creates a crystal. Each of us may feel himself unique, with an intrinsic destiny never before seen in the

universe . . . and yet to God we may be millions of crystals, identical in the eyes of the Cosmic Scientist. (*Shifting Realities* 186)

One should not, however, take Dick's somewhat bleak obituary to the human will here as gospel: like the literary naturalists before him, Dick finds the question of the relevance of the will in light of contemporary genetic, environmental, and cosmological theory an intriguing one, and worth exploring, but not dogma.

Psionic powers are often explained in science fiction, as in Dick's work, as the product of evolutionary development. Precognition, in particular, is a favorite psi device of Dick, and one finds it throughout his canon, from *The World Jones Made* to *Martian Time-Slip* to *Ubik*. Although not always the case, children are often the focal point for Dick's portrayal of psi powers, as in *Martian Time-Slip* and the short story "Jon's World." Children in Dick's fiction are frequently possessed of mystical (or near mystical) insight. They are artist figures and creators, and often symbolic of both innocence and knowledge in ways vaguely reminiscent of William Wordsworth's infants trailing clouds of glory. Because of their mystical abilities, children can be a powerful force in reshaping the way people view their environment, and even view themselves. In the short story "Piper in the Woods" (1953), for instance, workers on an asteroid begin to think they are plants, seemingly as a result of coming in contact with a young native girl living in the woods on the asteroid.

Evolutionary theory not only implies future development for the human species, but it also suggests the possibility for degeneration or devolution: the gradual return of an individual, a society, even a species, to prior—more primitive—evolutionary states. Evolutionary theory also suggests the possibility for atavistic reversals, in which traits present in the evolutionary history of a species—but long since overwritten by subsequent developments—surge to the surface and reassert themselves. For Dick, paranoia itself can be seen as an atavistic trait, a throwback to a more primitive state of human development.

One of Dick's best short stories, "The Golden Man" (1954), combines a tale built around the implications of evolutionary theory with issues of determinism, a critique of human nature, and the paranoia that emerges in the human encounter with the *other*. In this tale a government agency has been given the task of eradicating all "deeves," humans born with one of a wide variety of genetic mutations. Some of these genetic deviants have exceptional abilities—often connected with various psi powers—but they are also typically characterized by grotesque physical abnormalities. The mutants are relentlessly hunted down, captured, and euthanized by the government in an effort to prevent a species from evolving from human stock that will have superior survival skills and will, in time, eradicate the human race, in the same manner that (at least according to the tale) Cro-Magnon man replaced Neanderthal man. Thus, in order to prevent the human race from evolutionary irrelevance and eventual extinction, mutants are eliminated as quickly as possible, and prior to their reproduction if possible. Into this environment comes Cris Johnson, the golden man, a lion-maned "god" come to Earth. His genetic mutations leave him without humanlike intelligence or language ability, but give him the ability to "pre-think"—to see all possible futures and select the path most favorable to his own survival—as well as a sexual magnetism that gives him a decided advantage in the race to procreate. Cris's ability to "pre-think" raises issues of determinism, suggesting that an ability to eliminate randomness in one's future—

and thus eliminate others' free will in the sense that no willed act will be able to shake the pre-thinker's iron-clad future—gives him a survival advantage over those still caught in a web of indeterminacy. But even more intriguing, Dick's portrayal of human evolution in this tale runs counter to expectation and tradition, and is the focal point of the paranoia expressed by the government agents charged with eliminating Cris: human evolution produces not more advanced humans—with greater cognitive ability, according to the stereotypical portrayal—but a new species altogether, with superior survival skills in the evolutionary sense but with a distinct absence of *human* traits. Yet it is the paranoia of the human race, the same paranoia that has compelled the government to euthanize deeves as quickly as they can be identified, that may prove the key survival trait of the human race. If it were not for their paranoia, humans would stand no chance against the evolutionary *progress* of genetic deviation.

Technology, Media, Drugs, and Madness

Dick once observed that "information is the lifeblood, you know, the metabolism of the modern world."[44] As such, however, it is subject to manipulation, and to have the power to manipulate the lifeblood of modern civilization is to have the power to shape the appearance of reality itself. Technology and the media are the instruments most often used in Dick's world to shape how individuals view themselves and the society in which they participate. Knowledge that such manipulation is possible—yet occurs often outside of one's conscious awareness—leads to a lack of confidence in one's own ability to distinguish between the real and the unreal. Paranoia, therefore, is a common and proper response in Dick's world to the recognition that technology and the media are often under the direct control of forces, institutions, and agencies outside of one's control. As one critic notes, in many of Dick's works, such as *The Man Who Japed, Time Out of Joint, The Penultimate Truth,* and *The Simulacra,* the "media are controlled by a politically motivated power group, who effectively construct a false reality for the population."[45] Thus Dick's critique of the media examines both the manipulative power of advertising and media culture and a population that sacrifices free will when under the dazzling manipulations of the media. This dual critique is not necessarily a satire on the weakness of the human will, although it can be, for the agents who control the media in Dick's world are often in positions of political, intellectual, and/or spiritual power over the populace.

Throughout Dick's canon the proliferation of the media in American free-market enterprise serves as a grand metaphor for the simulacra that mediate the relationship between the human subject and external reality. An example of this can be found in *Ubik,* where Ubik manifests itself to the characters through media advertisements. Indeed in a technologically savvy, media-fueled world where simulacra stand as a barrier between the individual and the environment, the paraphernalia of culture can take on heightened ontological status through ubiquitous media glorification.[46] One finds characters in some of Dick's works, such as *Now Wait for Last Year* and *The Three Stigmata of Palmer Eldritch,* so conditioned to respond to their environment through simulacra that they will create their own simulated environments for entertainment. Sometimes the creation of these simulated environments is a matter not of entertainment but of psychological necessity, as in the short story "I Hope I Shall Arrive Soon" and *A Maze of Death.* In both of these works characters choose to enter virtual reality environments in order to keep from going mad from endless boredom and relentless claustrophobia on interminable—or near interminable—space flight. In the critically underappreciated *A Maze of Death,* the characters' voluntary submission to simulated realities becomes a meditation on the nature of reality, on the relevance and legitimacy of religious belief, and on the tension in human society between the veneer of civilization and primal urges toward violence.

One issue of importance for Dick raised by the proliferation of simulated realities concerns the epistemological confusion faced by those who want to separate the simulated—the fake, the inauthentic—from the real or authentic.[47] What constitutes authenticity—whether in a human being or in an environment or in an object—is a question with which Dick's characters often struggle. Dick's variations on this theme are legion. In both "We Can Remember It for You Wholesale" and "Imposter" the question is what constitutes authentic self-knowledge, and the difficulty for the central characters is in reconciling reality with memory, an issue raised again in the later novel *Do Androids Dream of Electric Sheep?* In other works, such as *Cosmic Puppets, Time Out of Joint, The Three Stigmata of Palmer Eldritch,* and *Flow My Tears, the Policeman Said,* characters are, in various ways, prevented from knowing the real, from experiencing authentic reality, by forces or agencies beyond their control and, in some cases, beyond their understanding entirely. In these works, in their quest for absolute reality, Dick's characters often have to negotiate the media and the agencies that direct and control the media.[48]

Sometimes in Dick's works one finds a clearly adversarial relationship between humankind and technology. In "The Great C" (1953), for instance, a devolved human tribe in a postapocalyptic world sacrifices humans to the Great C—a supercomputer that has found a way to sustain its power supply by converting human flesh into an energy source. Aside from the horrific relationship depicted here between humans and technology, the tale has clear epistemological implications: the Great C will stop demanding human sacrifice if the humans can devise a question that it cannot answer. In the tale, however, the human capacity to push the boundaries of intellectual investigation outward—particularly in their reduced tribal capacity—is no match for the all-encompassing knowledge of the computer. Thematically, therefore, this story suggests that the key to intellectual evolution rests in humankind's ability to think beyond the boundaries imposed by modern technological developments.

One "technology" that Dick's characters use, abuse, and attempt to come to terms with is drugs. Dick had a profound and pervasive interest in drugs, in part as a by-product of his own experimentation with them, and drug use of one form or another can be found in many of Dick's works, from recreational heroin use in *The World Jones Made* to the LSD visions of *Lies, Inc.* (revised from *The Unteleported Man*) to the reality-shaping effects of Chew-Z in *The Three Stigmata of Palmer Eldritch* and JJ-180 in *Now Wait for Last Year.* Within the context of most of his works, drugs are not advocated, generally speaking, primarily as a means for recreation; instead they operate metaphorically as a type of transformational technology that gives their users a perspective on contemporary civilization not available through normal sensory contact with the external world. They are, as in the famous scene in the film *The Matrix,* keys to the rabbit hole. This is not to suggest that the use of drugs by Dick or his characters reflects a mere "turn on, tune in, drop out" attitude toward drug-induced enlightenment. Far from it, in fact. Like, in another sense, psi powers in Dick's work, drugs are often presented as a means to merge technological development—metaphorically, if not literally—with human nature at the most fundamental level. Through psi powers and drugs, metaphorical technological enhancement is fully internalized within the subject. The result for the individual is a breakdown of normative reality. These breakdowns are sometimes positive—for they provide insight into the separation between authentic and inauthentic versions of reality, although, as in "Faith of Our Fathers," what is revealed as authentic can be a nightmare version of reality—but they are just as often negative, causing the individual to sink deeper into simulated versions of reality and to regress from the authentically real. Sometimes this regression is by choice, as in the players of the Perky Pat game in *The Three Stigmata of Palmer Eldritch,* and sometimes not, as in *Now Wait for Last Year* and *A Scanner Darkly.*

Perhaps more so than any other of his works, *A Scanner Darkly* explores the psychology of paranoia. In this novel technology—metaphorically through drug use, literally through the medium of the scramble suits and the police surveillance scanners—creates an environment in which personal identity fragments under the pressure of external conspiracy, shadowy power politics, and the despair that emerges from the individual's inability to make sense of his or her life. Dick noted in an interview that one "of the biggest transformations we have seen in human life in our society is the diminution of the sphere of the private. That we must reasonably now all regard the fact that there are no secrets and nothing is private. Everything is public."[49] The breakdown of the distinction between the private and the public induces paranoia through the realization that one is constantly under someone's watchful eye. This feeling, according to Dick, triggers within the individual a primal response: "Paranoia, in some respects, I think, is a modern-day development of an ancient, archaic sense that animals still have—quarry-type animals—that they're being watched"; thus paranoia is an "atavistic sense."[50] The answer to paranoia, Dick speculated, lay in the concept of *surprise:*

> Sudden surprises . . . are a sort of antidote to the paranoid . . . or, to be accurate about it, to live in such a way as to encounter sudden surprises quite often or even now and then [is] an indication that you are not paranoid, because to the paranoid, nothing is a surprise; everything happens exactly as he expected, and sometimes even more so. It all fits into his system. For us, though, there can be no system; maybe all systems—that is, any theoretical, verbal, symbolic, semantic, etc., formulation that attempts to act as an all-encompassing, all-explaining hypothesis of what the universe is about—are manifestations of paranoia. We should be content with the mysterious, the meaningless, the contradictory, the hostile, and most of all the unexplainably warm and giving.[51]

But for Dick's characters, making the choice to embrace surprise and stay content with uncertainty is virtually impossible. They, like Dick himself, are too often in pursuit of epiphany, in pursuit of authentic reality. More often than not, however, these quests lead characters to an awareness of the network of external forces and the forest of simulacra that create a barrier between the human and the absolute. Such encounters lead Dick's characters to the realization that their world is not what it seems, and they are not who they thought. Paranoia results, as characters lose their sense of identity and are consumed by forces beyond their understanding.[52]

Dick frequently drew on his own life experiences when crafting his novels, especially when it comes to exploring the tensions and complexities of human relationships and the mysteries of human spirituality. When it comes to drug use, as has been noted, Dick used and abused drugs throughout the 1960s. He did not often indulge in the more physically damaging and mentally deteriorating concoctions—amphetamines were his staple—but he did occasionally experiment with hallucinogens, although evidence suggests that he did so sparingly. Whatever romanticized view Dick may have taken regarding the Timothy Leary–esque potential of mind-altering substances, it all came crashing down in the early 1970s when Dick found himself with another broken marriage (number four at that time), a life filled with financial anxiety and existential paranoia, a home filled with burned-out nameless youth whose lives had been ruined by the excesses of the late 1960s, and a mind that occasionally wandered into thoughts of suicide (culminating in a near-fatal attempt on his own life in 1972). *A Scanner Darkly* is Dick's dark threnody to this period of his life.[53]

"In *A Scanner Darkly*," Dick once said in an interview, "I just tried to see how far you could push the terrible tragedies of the dope world: the hero's a narc who's reporting on himself and he's too burnt-out to know the difference anymore."[54] The title of the novel comes from St. Paul's first letter to the Corinthians (13:12) "For now we see through a glass, darkly; but then face to face: now I know in part, but then I shall know even as I am known." Dick alludes to this verse in several of his works, and nowhere is it more poignant than in this doppelgänger tale about the inability of the self to know itself. Literally the title refers to the holo-scanners in the novel, used by the narc Fred to spy on himself as Robert Arctor, and to the scramble suits worn by the narcs to protect their undercover identities. More important, however, the verse alludes in the novel to the profound inability of the disordered human mind to gain clarity in a world dominated by *mors ontologica,* by the death of the human spirit, the death of identity.

Dick was fascinated by the altered psychological state. Drugs, technology, and the media all, in Dick's world, contribute to the creation of the altered state of mind. Paranoia is the most prevalent response by Dick's characters to the pressures and manipulations of drugs, media, and technology, and as such paranoia is the most common of the extreme psychological states Dick explores. In fact paranoia is so prevalent throughout Dick's oeuvre that one might conclude that a degree of paranoia is—in the terms established by Dick's vast post–World War II cultural critique—a baseline psychological state and a perfectly normal and proper response to the pressures of contemporary sociopolitical culture. Beyond paranoia, Dick explores a wide variety of altered states of human consciousness—not all drug induced— and some of his works feature characters caught fully in the web of abnormal psychological states. From the cartoonish psychological obsessions of *Eye in the Sky* to the tragic psychological deterioration of Robert Arctor in *A Scanner Darkly* to the split-personality and manic-depressive disorders of *VALIS* to the suicidal melancholia of *The Transmigration of Timothy Archer,* Dick's works regularly investigate the human psychological response to contemporary culture, not just through baseline paranoia but through more extreme reactions as well. Whether these extreme psychological states deserve the epithet *mad* is an open question. Sometimes, as in *Clans of the Alphane Moon* (w. 1963–64, p. 1964), *madness* is a perfectly suitable term. But in other texts, such as *Martian Time-Slip*, schizophrenia is as much a window to altered categories of knowledge as it is a mark of human madness. In the final analysis, as with much good science fiction, Dick creates environments in his works that are different from the *real* world, but which simultaneously offer incisive critique of the *real*. The characters who inhabit Dick's world respond to it through altered and/or heightened psychological states, and are themselves set apart from the real through their paranoia, their madness, but who are at the same time keyed into the real in more meaningful ways than their sane counterparts. To be sane in a Dick work is to be deluded into placing trust in the ontological status of an illusory version of the real; to be mad is to reject the real on the path to ontological and epistemological enlightenment.

CHAPTER 5

Reading Philip K. Dick
Notes on Six Novels

There is no one way to read a Philip K. Dick novel. Each one poses its own riddles. Dick does have a certain set of thematic preoccupations—discussed previously—but it is not a narrow set, and Dick's treatment of these themes varies from narrative to narrative, even though some of his central convictions concerning the necessity of human empathy and the shifting nature of reality remain constant throughout. The six novels discussed below are considered to be among his greatest achievements. These works demonstrate the range of Dick's creative talents, the scope of his imagination, and the depth and breadth of his intellectual curiosity.

The Man in the High Castle

The Man in the High Castle (w. 1961, p. 1962), the only Dick work to win the Hugo Award,[1] is an alternative history novel—or, arguably, an alternate universe novel—in which the United States and its allies have lost World War II, and the continental United States has been divided into three regions: Germany has taken control of the eastern half of the United States, Japan has control of the Pacific coastal states, and the Rocky Mountain states represent a thin, neutral barrier between the two in which relatively free citizens negotiate a tension-filled life for themselves. The novel is better labeled speculative fiction as opposed to science fiction; the conventional devices of science fiction are absent, and the novel is entirely an exercise in speculation stemming from the question, *what if the Allies lost World War II?* The result of this exercise is a work with multiple overlapping plot lines and impressive, realistic characterization that is a significant step forward from the apprenticeship works of the 1950s in terms of narrative and philosophical complexity. This complexity has attracted considerable scholarly attention: more has been written about *The Man in the High Castle* than any other Dick novel.[2]

The Man in the High Castle is driven by contrasts and oppositions. The Nazis remain fascist and totalitarian in governmental structure and driven by a fierce will toward expansion and domination, pushing their genocidal ethnic cleansing into successively newer territories. In contrast, the Japanese seem relatively benevolent, despite their occupation of the Pacific states. They are ruled by different passions than their Nazi counterparts, and search for wisdom in the *I Ching* and in Taoism rather than in the German will to power.[3] Prior to the beginning of the novel, the Nazis have already turned the continent of Africa into a wasteland with their Aryan ambitions, and, as one discovers in the course of the novel, a group within the German power structure has set its sights on the elimination of the Japanese as well. In order to maximize their power and limit their losses, the Germans, one discovers, are planning a surprise attack on the Japanese. This conflict is the key to one of the primary plot lines of the novel, and one of the main characters, Nobusuke Tagomi, becomes a central figure in the efforts of a subversive German political group to get word, covertly, to the Japanese authorities that the German strike is being planned. Political power struggles predominate in *The Man in the High Castle,* and behind the overt political maneuvering one finds a philosophical tension between Taoism and fascism and between individual freedom and totalitarianism. The human will is the central actor in these tensions: the totalitarian will to power is set against the Taoist submission of the will; the will to individual freedom is set against the fascist abandonment of the individual will to the glory of the state.[4]

This conflict between Taoism and fascism is more than just a commentary on conflicting ideologies. The totalitarian will to power that fuels the imperialistic ethnic cleansing of the Nazis is quite clearly a product of metaphysical evil. The cant sputtered forth from Hitler, the text points out, was the product of a diseased mind, and yet it became the "Holy Writ" of the Nazi movement—which spread itself, like an infectious disease, around the world. Dick writes that the views of the Nazis "had infected a civilization by now, and, like evil spores, the blind blond Nazi queens were swishing out from Earth to the other planets, spreading the contamination." The philosophical inbreeding of Nazi ideologues is a symbolic incest, and the consequences of incest are "madness, blindness, death" (36).[5] The disregard and disconnection with humanity—a lack of empathy for one's fellow humans—perpetuate this evil ideology among the Nazis and their sympathizers. They are pursuing an abstract ideology without any regard for the real-world implications of their ideology for their fellow humans.[6] The Nazis' blindness to the real world and real individuals is a product of their desire to transform the world into their image. As Baynes—the covert German agent sent to San Francisco to warn the Japanese of the German plot to destroy them—concludes regarding Nazi imperialism: "They want to be the agents, not the victims, of history. They identify with God's power and believe they are godlike. That is their basic madness. They are overcome by some archetype; their egos have expanded psychotically so that they cannot tell where they begin and the godhead leaves off. It is not hubris, not pride; it is inflation of the ego to its ultimate—confusion between him who worships and that which is worshipped. Man has not eaten God; God has eaten man." What they fail to see "is man's *helplessness*" and thus cannot engage their fellow humans with empathy, with kindness (41–42).

As a counter to the egomaniacal Nazis and their God-complex, the central characters in *High Castle* are one by one brought to moments of crisis when they choose—through an act of individual will—to demonstrate empathy and act for the benefit of their fellow humans rather than for the benefit of an ideological imperative. In so choosing, they find a degree of liberation.[7] Tagomi's slaying of the German agents sent to kill the Japanese general Tedeki and his later signing for the release of Frank Frink (whom the Germans wanted to deport and, presumably, execute, for Frink is Jewish); Juliana's slaying of the assassin (Joe Cinnadella) sent to kill the author of *The Grasshopper Lies Heavy,* Hawthorne Abendsen (whose alternative history novel about a world in which the Allies won World War II is deemed subversive by the German government); and even, in its own way, the surprising demand of the often unlikable art dealer Childan that a Japanese man apologize for insinuating that American art is worth little more than to become the object of a mass-market fad—all are moments in which characters reject the pressures of oppressive ideology and choose individual acts rooted in human empathy.

Another opposition that operates thematically throughout the novel is the distinction between the *authentic* and the *inauthentic,* or the real and the fake.[8] Nobusuke Tagomi is a dealer in historical American cultural artifacts—objects collected primarily by wealthy Japanese families and professionals. The value of the artifacts is largely a function of their authenticity (a generalization that leads to major plot developments in the narrative as it is revealed that companies often make a fortune by mass producing fake artifacts and selling them as legitimate). The concept of authenticity is slippery, however, for, as one character in the novel demonstrates, authenticity is not a quality inherent in the artifact itself—it is a characteristic ascribed to an artifact by external sources that validate the object's authenticity. Thus the "word 'fake' meant nothing really, since the word 'authentic' meant nothing really" (64). Without a certificate of authenticity proving that a cigarette lighter was once owned by Franklin Delano Roosevelt, for example, it has no more value than any other lighter. But with that certificate, it is—according to the mysterious logic of commodity fetishization—more valuable. Its historicity has been validated.

By merging the concept of authenticity with the related concept of historicity, *High Castle*'s role as an alternative history novel is itself a part of the overall thematic structure of the work. Just as an artifact receives its value as an object of history through an external authenticating instrument—it has no special inherent value in this case—so, too, does history require an authenticating document—the historical narrative itself—in order to find its preservation and validation. As an alternative history, *High Castle* functions as a text validating a certain version of history. The alternative history within the alternative history—*The Grasshopper Lies Heavy*—is a mirror image of *High Castle,* and the mirroring of these two works serves to highlight their own lack of authenticity: they are both false versions of the real. When Juliana interprets the *I Ching* at the home of Abendsen to mean that history as she has experienced it is an illusion and that the version of history presented in *Grasshopper* is authentic, she is right, but she might be missing the larger point: the "inner truth" of the novel is that these twinned histories are no more valid than any other artifact that derives its value not from within itself but from some external, authenticating document. Thus, as a work of *meta*fiction, *High Castle* is a statement about artistic creation itself and the tension inherent in ascribing value and authenticity to a work of art.

There is, however, a way out of the recursive loop created by the mirroring of *High Castle* and *Grasshopper,* and that can be found in the concept of *wu.* The object with *wu,* as the young Japanese businessman Paul explains to Childan while discussing a piece of jewelry fashioned by Frank Frink, has its own authenticity: its value is inherent within itself and does not require an external source of validation. As a new thing, as an inherently authentic creation, the piece of jewelry points toward "a new world"—one outside the mirrored worlds of *High Castle* and *Grasshopper* (see 175–77). There is no question of authenticity about Frank Frink's jewelry: it simply *is* authentic. As Childan remarks when he first elects to sell Frink's jewelry on consignment, "*With these, there's no problem of authenticity*" (147).

Late in the novel the reader is given a brief glimpse, through the eyes of Tagomi, of the "new world" that Frink's *wu*-infused jewelry points toward. Distraught over his seemingly righteous but emotionally troubling slaying of the German assassins, Tagomi seeks comfort in a piece of Frink's jewelry—which Childan had presented to him As he stares into the silver artifact, he sees not through a glass darkly, but he sees and experiences directly, for a few brief moments, the real world—the actual, modern San Francisco of Philip K. Dick and the reader of *High Castle.* It is a disturbing, hellish, tomb-world for Tagomi, though it is a world the reader of *High Castle* readily recognizes as his or her own, and Tagomi retreats from it quickly. It is a "Mad dream,

Mr. Tagomi thought. Must wake up. Where are the pedcabs today? He began to walk faster. Whole vista has dull, smoky, tomb-world cast. Smell of burning. Dim gray buildings, sidewalk, peculiar harsh tempo in people. And *still* no pedcabs. . . . Only cars and buses. Cars like brutal big crushers, all unfamiliar in shape. He avoided seeing them; kept his eyes straight ahead. Distortion of my optic perception of particularly sinister nature" (231). This is a nightmare landscape for Tagomi—and, seeing it (darkly, perhaps?) through Tagomi's eyes, it may seem as such to the reader—but it is merely a snapshot of the real world, the actual San Francisco of the early 1960s. To Tagomi, it is horrific in comparison with the familiar landscape of *his* world in *The Man in the High Castle* As a metafictional work, therefore, *High Castle* suggests that all narrative histories are to a degree idealized versions of the real, against which the real itself seems a diminished thing.

The Man in the High Castle is one of Dick's most accomplished works. It is a commentary on political power, on the nature of history, on value, and on the necessity of human empathy and responsibility in the face of fascist and totalitarian evil.[9] As a social critique, *High Castle* is an indictment of racism. As political commentary, it asks the reader to consider ways in which the authentic American political experience is itself tainted by power politics and elements of fascism and totalitarianism. As a commentary on art and artisanship, *High Castle* is one of Dick's most provocative and challenging works on the complex interplay of art and the artificer, and of the relationship between the authentic and the inauthentic in art and history.

Martian Time-Slip

One of several novels by Dick that take place in whole or in part on Mars, *Martian Time-Slip* highlights many of Dick's preoccupations in the early 1960s.[10] Although not received with the same fanfare and recognition as *The Man in the High Castle*, *Martian Time-Slip* is every bit its equal in terms of quality of writing, and as a vehicle for the exploration of ideas, it blends together several of Dick's key themes. It is one of Dick's most successful blendings of political and economic commentary with metaphysical musings about the nature of the universe.[11]

In his essay "Drugs, Hallucinations, and the Quest for Reality," published the same year as *Martian Time-Slip*, Dick explores the implications of Kantian epistemological theory when it comes to understanding the apparent disconnect from the *real* that one finds among individuals with mental illness.[12] Kant argued that one did not view the objects of external reality, of *beings in-themselves*, directly: the faculties of the individual human mind organize the flood of sensory data (a flood that would overwhelm the individual if not filtered and shaped first by the perceiving mind) received through the senses into an intellectually manageable stream of information. Because this process of organization occurs within the individual human mind, no two individuals can be sure that they perceive external reality in precisely the same way. Moreover under normal circumstances no individual truly sees objective reality—in Dick's world one almost always sees reality through a glass darkly, and one of the implications of Kantian epistemology is that some of the darkness in the glass stems from the fact that what we perceive is also filtered through the shaping and organizing faculties of the individual mind. In light of this, Dick speculates in his essay, perhaps people with mental illness are not so much disconnected from the real but, on the contrary, are overconnected to the real: some of the filters separating the subjective perceiver from the real have been removed, and the subsequent flood of the real into the mind of the individual results in what appears to those still seeing through dark glass as madness. Schizophrenia, the dominant mental illness among Dick's characters, may not separate one from perceived reality, but may actually be evidence of an individual's confrontation of the truly *real*. Encounters with the real, however, are often terrifying in Dick's world: the organizing faculties of the mind may be saving one from the fundamental horrors of the universe.

Unfortunately an encounter with *being-in-itself*—with the "unshared" world—and the seeming madness that results, often lead to social alienation for the individual. As Dick writes in this essay, "Real or unreal . . . the unshared world that we call 'hallucinatory' is destructive: Alienation, isolation, a sense of everything being strange, of things altering and bending—all this is the logical result, until the individual, formerly a part of human culture, becomes an organic 'windowless monad'" (173). This is the state in which the reader finds Manfred Steiner in *Martian Time-Slip*. Warehoused in a facility for physically and mentally abnormal children—and deemed disposable by many in society as a result—the autistic Manfred is completely isolated from the rest of society, a fact that helps drive Manfred's father, Norbert Steiner, to suicide early in the novel. Manfred's utter isolation from society is less a function of madness, per se, but is a function of his perception of a higher and broader version of reality (of *reality in-itself*) Manfred simply sees more than the other characters in the novel. In one scene, as Jack Bohlen views the holographic teaching machines at the local school, he observes that the

> entire Public School was geared to a task which went contrary to his grain: the school was there not to inform or educate, but to mold, and along severely limited lines. It was the link to their inherited culture, and it peddled that

culture, in its entirety, to the young. It bent its pupils to it; perpetuation of the culture was the goal, and any special quirks in the children which might lead them in another direction had to be ironed out.

It was a battle, Jack realized, between the composite psyche of the school and the individual psyches of the children, and the former held all the key cards. A child who did not properly respond was assumed to be autistic—that is, oriented according to a subjective factor that took precedence over his sense of objective reality. And that child wound up by being expelled from the school; he went, after that, to another sort of school entirely, one designed to rehabilitate him: he went to Camp Ben-Gurion. He could not be taught; he could only be dealt with as ill. (72–73)

Thus, Jack speculates, autism, or schizophrenia, meant a "person who could not live out the drives implanted in him by his society" (73). Seen in this manner, Manfred is ill only insofar as he has not incorporated a vision of reality that is a learned, shared cultural inheritance. Instead, he sees reality at a level deeper than the linear, time-constricted version of the real perceived in common by society. But because what he sees is uncommon, language fails for Manfred as a tool of human interaction. Language, Dick points out in "Drugs, Hallucinations, and the Quest for Reality," is an essential human tool because it helps humans establish a semblance of commonality in their perceptions of the external world. When, as in Manfred's case, the overperceiving individual attempts to communicate, there is "breakdown of the shared language," but the "overperception emanates from outside the organism; the percept system of the organism is perceiving what is actually there, and it should not be doing so, because to do so is to make the cognitive process impossible, *however real the entities perceived are.* The problem actually seems to be that rather than 'seeing what isn't there' the organism is seeing what *is* there—but no one else does, hence no semantic sign exists to depict the entity and therefore the organism cannot continue an empathic relationship with the members of his society" (173).

Throughout most of the novel, the one word Manfred is able to speak is the seemingly nonsensical *gubble*. This word communicates nothing to the other characters in the novel, but that is because, as a semantic sign, gubble refers to something in the real, not something in the shared language world of linear time experienced by the other characters. What Manfred sees are the unseen entropic forces of the universe pushing everything toward decay, and gubble is both the semantic symbol for the breakdown of common language and the literal desiderata of entropic decay itself. Manfred's world is a world of horrors, and the few times the reader is allowed to see from Manfred's viewpoint, the vision is is always of a nightmare world of rapid decay. When the reader is first introduced to Manfred's view of the world, the imagery is startling, grotesque, and surreal:

> High in the sky circled meat-eating birds. At the base of the windowed building lay their excrement. He picked up the wads until he held several. They twisted and welled like dough, and he knew there were living creatures within; he carried them carefully into the empty corridor of the building. One wad opened, parted with a split in its woven, hair-like side; it became too large to hold, and he saw it now in the wall. A compartment where it lay on its side, the rent so wide that he perceived the creature within.
>
> Gubbish! A worm, coiled up, made of wet, bony-white pleats, the inside gubbish worm, from a person's body. If

only the high-flying birds could find it and eat it down, like that. He ran down the steps, which gave beneath his feet. Boards missing. He saw down through the sieve of wood to the soil beneath, the cavity, dark, cold, full of wood so rotten that it lay in damp powder, destroyed by gubbish-rot. (129)

This vision is a subversive undercutting of the optimism of the novel's other characters: Manfred's ability to perceive time flowing at a rate far faster than normal is the coeval of the psychiatrist Milton Glaub's time-compressed film of a germinating seed. But Manfred sees decay, not birth, the sterility of the tomb world, not the fertility of a natural world in bloom. Like the Martian landscape itself, Manfred's visions are of a dry and dusty world.

Visions are key to *Martian Time-Slip*. Indeed the concept of speculation, of seeing, ties the metaphysical and epistemological themes to the novel's political and economic themes For instance, the land speculation of Leo Bohlen and Arnie Kott is a form of economic foresight—a seeing into future economic circumstances. Similarly relationships are the subject of speculation, as characters in the novel have affairs, deceive one another, and sexually exploit each other in attempts to secure emotional stability in the midst of economic and political pressures. Characters cast about for relations with high-yield reward in a manner that loosely parallels the land speculation of Leo Bohlen and Arnie Kott. Connected to the concept of speculation is the exploitation motif, which Dick explores in a variety of ways throughout the novel. Economic exploitation is central to the activities of both Leo Bohlen and Arnie Kott, who attempt in different ways to exploit a capitalist free market through aggressive—and arguably unethical—real estate speculation.

Otto Zitte's use of his door-to-door black market sales business as a means to seduce lonely women—whether married or not—suggests a certain type of sexual exploitation. Racial exploitation is exhibited in the treatment of the indigenous Martians—the Bleekmen—who are either left beggars in the barren wilderness or are reduced to servant roles for the merchant-class colonists. Indeed Arnie Kott's unapologetically racist use of the term *nigger* in reference to the Bleekman highlights the racial exploitation Dick is exposing in the novel. A corollary of the racial exploitation in the novel can be found in the treatment of malformed or mentally challenged children in the novel: society would rather warehouse and destroy these children than have to admit their existence. Acknowledging their existence would force procolonizing political interests to deal with the unpleasant public relations challenge of having to promote space colonization despite evidence that such travel may elevate the potential for genetic deviation in one's offspring. Finally, one finds Dick exploring the exploitation of the human psyche, as Arnie Kott attempts to break through Manfred's autism in order to exploit the child's ability to see the future. Kott has no regard for the child—his only regard is for the knowledge Manfred has that Kott can use for his own economic gain. Manfred is a mere commodity in Kott's economic schemes.

The answer to exploitation is empathy, and the answer to entropy is repair. In a world where life-giving water is a precious commodity, the wastefulness of Arnie Kott's steam shower is another manifestation of exploitation—this time of natural resources. But Kott's reluctance in the novel to give a group of dying, dehydrated Bleekman wandering through the desert any water exhibits a profound lack of empathy. Meanwhile Jack Bohlen's uncomplaining gift of water to the Bleekman, as well as, in a larger sense, his job as a repairman—a job of considerable symbolic importance in Dick's world, as has been discussed earlier in this study—serves as a hopeful contrast to Kott's wastefulness and disregard of his fellow humans—or Bleekmen, as the case may be.

The entropic world that is opened to Manfred—and, at times, to Jack Bohlen, who struggles with his own schizophrenic urges throughout the novel, urges that manifested themselves when Jack was a young adult but which he subsequently repressed, only to have them reassert themselves through his interaction with Manfred—is a world ruled by deterministic pressures. In the entropic world, the organic world is revealed to be a mechanistic world in which the natural world and human endeavor are subverted by the destructive and coercive forces of the universe. In the "shared language" world of normative reality, the world of human endeavor is mythologized as a world of freedom, growth, and choice, but this may be mere hopeful illusion constructed by the individual and shared with others through language. But—as Jack witnessed when his schizophrenia first revealed itself in a horrific vision of the mechanized interior of another human—the world of the *idios kosmos* and the world of the *koinos kosmos* often bear little relation to each other. In the world of *Martian Time-Slip*, it is possible that hopeful speculations about the freedom of the individual are mere *gubble*.

Now Wait for Last Year

The school of thought that argues that science fiction must be scientifically plausible has little patience for *Now Wait for Last Year* (w. 1963, p. 1966). The array of time paradoxes and intersecting parallel universes in this novel resists logical explanation. But similar criticisms might be leveled against any number of

Dick's other novels, and if one finds the seeming logical inconsistencies in the plot a barrier against appreciation, let alone interpretation, then one misses the point. Dick's universes are always a bit more mysterious, a bit more irrational, than otherwise. To the extent that the postmodern universe is one that transcends the rational logic of a prequantum world, *Now Wait for Last Year* is clearly a postmodern novel. As Dick made evident throughout his career, the universe is a chaotic place and defies neat categorization, particularly when one factors in human subjectivity.[13] Besides, Dick wrote novels not just to embody weighty themes but to entertain. After all, entertainment—regardless of its adherence to the decorum of rationality—pays the bills with far more regularity than philosophy.

Most of the logical conundrums in *Now Wait for Last Year* stem from the introduction of the drug JJ-180 into the plot. This drug—which is lethally addictive upon a single use—causes its user to move through time. The effect is not the same for everyone: some move backward in time, some forward, and some laterally into alternative versions of the present. Each of the central players in the novel reacts differently. Kathy Sweetscent travels backward in time; her husband, Eric Sweetscent, travels forward in time; and the leader of Terra, the dictator Gino Molinari (aka the Mole), moves laterally. There is some debate among the characters in the novel regarding whether users of JJ-180 *really* time travel, or if they only experience time travel as a drug-induced hallucination—but events in the novel make it difficult to "explain" everything away as pure hallucination. Nevertheless the dizzying effects of time travel in the novel—including the meeting of oneself in the future (as Eric does), the reshaping of the present by manipulating the past (as Kathy attempts), and the alliance of multiple selves in parallel universes toward a common goal in one universe (as Molinari affects)—are used by Dick to explore the nature and meaning of human ethics. *Now Wait for Last Year* is a novel about human choices in a chaotic world: in a world of cynicism, hatred, loneliness, and oppression, in which human choices multiply with the splintering of linear time, sometimes ethical human behavior is determined more by what we choose *not* to do as opposed to what we do.

In the novel Terra finds itself caught in the middle of an interstellar war between the Starmen of Lilistar and the Reegs of the Proxima System. Because human life on Terra descended from Lilistar colonists eons ago, the Terrans and Starmen bear close physical resemblance. The Reegs, however, resemble bugs The common ancestry shared by the Starmen and the Terrans results in an unholy alliance: Molinari, in an effort to preserve Terra, forms an alliance with the Starmen in their ongoing war with the Reegs. Unfortunately physical resemblance and common ancestry do not result in mutual regard, and the Starmen infiltrate Terra and seek to use it and its people for their own purposes. The Reegs, despite their antlike appearance, have no desire to use and manipulate the people of Terra. Molinari, realizing his mistake in forging an alliance with the wrong side in the interstellar conflict, is forced to take on unending physical ailments both as a type of repentance and as a form of complex diplomacy that keeps the Starmen from taking more aggressive steps to place Terra under the thumb of domination.

Dick based Molinari on Mussolini, whom Dick believed was an otherwise well-intentioned and strong leader who made the mistake of forging an alliance with the devil.[14] The comparison may not be particularly apt in the reader's eyes. The question for Dick, however, is that having made such an alliance, how should one respond? The ethical nature of Molinari's response is to wear his guilt as a cloak of physical ailments, ailments that have the added effect of preventing the Starmen from making quicker work of the process of bringing Terra under complete subjection.

All of this political intrigue is secondary in the novel to the story of the marriage of Kathy and Eric Sweetscent. There is no love lost between them, and Eric would like nothing more than to divorce Kathy and be set free. Kathy, for all of her hatred for her husband, does not want divorce: psychologically Kathy needs the stabilizing presence of Eric in order for her to cope with the pressures of life. Kathy finds some relief from these pressures in drugs, and this quest for relief results in her addiction to JJ-180. The central question of the novel for Eric is what he should do about Kathy. As difficult as their relationship was prior to JJ-180, it is worse afterward, for the drug has caused permanent brain damage in Kathy (the extent and implications of which are never quite clarified in the novel, and Kathy remains alert and communicative throughout), and his marriage—already an unhappy one—now has nothing to offer him but a lifetime of having to care for a woman who alternately loves and hates him and who offers little in the way of joy, comfort, or mature companionship. Eric's struggle with his responsibilities to Kathy and Molinari's struggle with his responsibilities to the people of Terra are the parallel psychological dramas that make up the thematic core of the novel. In these two situations, what is the ethical thing to do? What does it mean to be good?[15] These questions come to a point at the very end of the novel. In the work's concluding scene, Eric has a conversation with the autocab in which he is traveling:

> To the cab he said suddenly, "If your wife were sick—"
> "I have no wife, sir," the cab said. "Automated Mechanisms never marry; everyone knows that."

"All right," Eric agreed. "If you were me, and your wife were sick, desperately so, with no hope of recovery, would you leave her? Or would you stay with her, even if you had traveled ten years into the future and knew for an absolute certainty that the damage to her brain could never be reversed? And staying with her would mean—"

"I can see what you mean, sir," the cab broke in. "It would mean no other life for you beyond caring for her."

"That's right," Eric said.

"I'd stay with her," the cab decided.

"Why?"

"Because," the cab said, "life is composed of reality configurations so constituted. To abandon her would be to say, I can't endure reality as such. I have to have uniquely special easier conditions."

"I think I agree," Eric said after a time. "I think I will stay with her."

"God bless you, sir," the cab said. "I can see that you're a good man."

"Thank you," Eric said.[16]

Eric acts ethically toward Kathy by accepting reality for what it is—rather than seeking what is was or what it could be—and by choosing not to act, not to divorce his wife. The title of the novel emphasizes the human desire to escape present reality by retreating to idealized versions of the past: we spend our days avoiding the harsh realities of the present by waiting for a return to the better times of last year. There is an inherent futility is such desires, and *Now Wait for Last Year* is, in this regard, a bleak novel. Its moments of dark humor are not tempered by the madcap lunacy of another novel of marital antagonism, *Clans of the Alphane Moon*, which Dick wrote right after *Now Wait for Last Year*. The lengths that characters will go in *Now Wait for Last*

Year to avoid present reality range from taking drugs to building detailed life-size models of past environments—such as Virgil Ackerman's Wash-35 (Washington, D.C., 1935)—in which to escape from the present. The value of Eric's decision to stay with Kathy at the end of the novel stems from his willingness to forego the dreams of yesteryear and to live life in the present without the crutch of "uniquely special easier conditions." In a world in which time has fractured and people can, under the influence of JJ-180, travel into the past, into the future, or even sideways into alternate, parallel realities, to accept the present moment for what it is constitutes a kind of centering of the self rarely seen in Dick's work.

Paradoxically, in order to have the moral fortitude to live in the present reality without trying to escape into idealized versions of the past, alternative versions of the present, or hopeful conditions of the future, one must root one's sense of self in that which is timeless. This is the message Eric takes from his encounter with the Lazy Brown Dog carts. These simple mechanical life forms—fashioned out of pity by the humble artisan Bruce Himmel—strive to live their modest lives and to avoid destruction at the hands of the more powerful. For Eric, the Lazy Brown Dog carts become a living parable of the basic needs and drives of existence. After having observed a cart a decade into the future cowering in a pail, Eric thinks to himself, "Strange . . . that in the center of the greatest abomination of our times, this war, I should find something meaningful. A desire animating me equal to that possessed by the Lazy Brown Dog cart hiding in the zinc pail ten years from now. Maybe I'm its compatriot at last. Able to take my place in the world beside it, do as it does, fight as it fights: whenever it's necessary and then some, for the pleasure of it. For the joy. As was intended from the start, anterior to any time or condition I could comprehend or call my own or enter into" (228). For Eric the core of one's identity is rooted in a value system anterior to any time or condition, and which allows one to live an ethical life in the present reality. In this manner one may live in the moment without endlessly waiting for the arrival of last year.

The Three Stigmata of Palmer Eldritch

Several things in Dick's life converged in the months just prior to drafting *The Three Stigmata of Palmer Eldritch*.[17] In late 1963 and early 1964 Dick witnessed his daughters playing with Barbie and Ken dolls, and as a result was inspired to write the short story "The Days of Perky Pat" (1963), which tells of survivors of an interplanetary war on a defeated, destroyed, and desolate Earth who spend their time playing elaborate games using "Perky Pay Layouts"—Barbie-size miniatures of a prewar Earth. Meanwhile Dick's marriage to his third wife, Anne, was in its waning months (they would separate in 1964 and divorce in 1965), and, as part of their sunset efforts to find marital peace, they had started to attend an Episcopalian church. This spurred Dick's already considerable interest in theology, and his fascination with the mysteries of orthodox Christianity—including the nature of communion and the doctrine of transubstantiation, the meaning of baptism, the nature of sin and evil, the doctrine of the trinity—was fueled by his association with the church. In addition, during this period Dick was writing at a white-hot pace (drafting some ten novels in little more than a year's time), and was doing much of this while taking amphetamines in order to sustain the long stretches of time he spent writing each day. In 1963, in the middle of this intense period of his life—but what periods of Dick's life were not intense?—Dick had a vision: "I looked up at the sky and saw a face. I didn't really see it, but the face was there, and it was not a human face; it was a vast visage of perfect evil. . . . It was immense; it filled a quarter of the sky. It had empty slots for eyes—it was metal and cruel and, worst of all, it was God."[18] He would soon give this vision a name: Palmer Eldritch. *Three Stigmata* is a novel in which Dick pulls together all of these influences. It is a novel about Christian mysteries, about the emotional torment of a failed marriage, about adults seeking refuge from despair through the use of Barbie and Ken surrogates, and about a vision of mechanized evil in the form of the larger-than-life Palmer Eldritch.

In *Three Stigmata,* a story of corporate competition between rival drug pushers takes on serious theological significance. In order to escape the daily despair of their lives in the wasteland of Mars, colonists take an illegal drug, Can-D. This drug causes its users to enter the world of Perky Pat and Walt (modeled after Barbie and Ken dolls, respectively). Under the influence of the drug, the colonists are translated into the world of the "layout"—a scale version of an idealized, fantasy Earth setting in which Perky Pat and her male companion live their untroubled lives. The layouts themselves are not illegal, and an entire industry (monopolized by Perky Pat Layouts, a company owned and operated by Leo Bulero) has developed in order to supply the colonists with these miniaturized toy settings. Craftspeople— such as the pot designer Emily Hnatt and her salesman/husband, Richard—make their living by selling products to Perky Pat Layouts in order to be "minned"—miniaturized in order to fit the world of Perky Pat in scale. But, and here is where *Three Stigmata* differs considerably from the short story "The Days of Perky Pat," the true value of the layouts for the colonists on Mars is only realized through the use of Can-D. The translation of the Can-D users into the world of Perky Pat is considered by many on Mars to be a genuine religious experience: it is perceived as a kind of metempsychosis or transmigration of the soul, and some argue that the user is literally translated into the body of Perky Pat on Earth—or an idealized version of Earth— while others believe that the translation is only figurative, not literal, and is only valuable as a type of hallucinatory escapism. The experience of translation is fleeting, and ends the moment the Can-D wears off, but the world one experiences is idealized—at least, in a shallow, postcard-style—and thus gives the colonists brief respite from the dust and decay of Mars. It is a taste of heaven for the colonists, a little salvation. In Dick's world, to be saved is, in effect, to be preserved from the forces of entropy and decay; as one character suggests in *Three Stigmata*, in a state of Can-D-induced translation, the user is placed in an environment not subject to decay, and the user has "put on immortality" (47).[19] Late in the novel, a new émigré to Mars, Anne Hawthorne, invokes Pauline doctrine in order to describe the process of the soul's ascension out of the realm of entropic decay. As Hawthorne notes, the corruptible human puts on incorruptibility "[St.] Paul says our enemy is death; it's the final enemy we overcome, so I guess it's the greatest. We're all blighted, according to Paul, not just our bodies but our souls, too; both have to die and then we can be born again, with new bodies not of flesh but incorruptible" (148). Taking Can-D is the closest a living human can come to having to this experience, notes Anne.[20] But is the experience of the users genuine—is it *real*—or is it mere effect, a pleasant illusion that allows brief refuge from the real?

For Dick, the theological implications of this question are legion. In *Three Stigmata* the debate over the relative reality of the experience of the users of Can-D invokes centuries of theological speculation over the doctrine of transubstantiation and the nature and meaning of communion: do the wafer and wine truly partake of the substance of the body and blood of Christ? One Can-D user, Sam Regan, is a believer: "He affirmed the miracle of translation—the near-sacred moment in which the miniature artifacts of the layout no longer merely represented Earth but *became* Earth. And he and the others, joined together in the fusion of doll-inhabitation by means of the Can-D, were transported outside of time and local space. Many of the colonists were as yet unbelievers; to them the layouts were merely symbols of a world which none of them could any longer experience. But, one by one, the unbelievers came around" (37). As Sam observes, the consumption of Can-D is itself done in communal fashion, and the language of religious experience permeates the novel. In addition, the mystery of the Trinity is evoked, for the communal users of Can-D are translated into a doll of the same sex: if three males take Can-D together, they are all translated into the same Walt doll, and their psyches must act in harmony in order to accomplish anything during the fleeting moments of the translation experience (the three are distinct and separate, yet they are *one Walt* in the world of the layout).

Because the experience of using Can-D is fleeting, a rival drug emerges, Chew-Z, which promises to deliver what Can-D cannot: a lasting experience of eternal life. Chew-Z, brought back to Earth's solar system from Proxima—a distant solar system in the galaxy—by Palmer Eldritch, is sold to the public with the extravagant advertising claim, "GOD PROMISES ETERNAL LIFE. WE CAN DELIVER IT" (150). As both Leo Bulero and Barney Mayerson discover upon taking Chew-Z—Leo involuntarily, Barney voluntarily—the world one is translated to is dominated by the presence of Palmer Eldritch, who manipulates the landscape at whim, and with malevolent effect.

Eldritch is a curious and sinister figure. He is a larger-than-life entrepreneur whose exploits have been followed closely by the public, but as the novel begins he has been absent from Earth's solar system for a decade, lost, presumably, in the midst of conducting business in the Proxima system. He has three physical peculiarities, three "stigmata": an artificial arm, metal teeth, and mechanical eyes. His is an imposing, even horrifying presence, and, as a result, Eldritch is readily recognizable by the populace. As the reader comes to discover, at some point during his decade absence Eldritch has been—or might have been—taken over or possessed by a godlike alien force. This force has ambitions to preserve itself by taking over—by figuratively consuming—the human populations on Earth and Mars. Chew-Z is a catalyst for this takeover, and takers of Chew-Z—as witnessed during the labyrinthian struggles of Barney Mayerson and Leo Bulero to overcome Eldritch in the last third of the novel—find themselves manifesting the stigmata of Eldritch himself.

So in one sense *Three Stigmata* is a novel about an alien invasion, but to read it solely that way is to miss the genius of the novel, for the alien may or may not be a god, and the takeover may or may not be a literalization of the theological drama of salvation and damnation. The tensions in the novel are propelled not so much by the alien invasion story as by the metaphysical and theological issues raised by the shape-shifting realities experienced by the characters under the influence of Can-D and Chew-Z. Dick relies on the language of medieval ontological theory in his description of the mysteries of translation in *Three Stigmata* He distinguishes, as many medieval scholars did, between substance (the essence of being) and accident (the particulars of being). When Leo Bulero—under the influence of Chew-Z—encounters a young girl and asks her if she is really Palmer Eldritch, the girl says: "Take the medieval doctrine of substance versus accidents. . . . My accidents are those of this child, but my substance, as with the wine and the wafer in transubstantiation—" (91). Eldritch is the substance, just as are the blood and body of Christ in the communion ritual; the physical manifestation of the girl, as with the physical wine and wafer, are accidental—they are the particular manifestations of the ontological essence of Eldritch and of Christ.

But Eldritch is no Christ—he is more antimessiah than messiah. To understand Eldritch one must understand some of the basic elements of Gnosticism. As was discussed in chapter 4, Dick found Gnosticism a compelling theological system. In *Three Stigmata* the Gnostic belief that the creator of the world of experience is a secondary and flawed god helps position Eldritch within the ideological framework of the narrative. Eldritch is evil in the cosmic flawed-god sense of evil—the Gnostic Archon or demiurge sense—but is not entirely evil in the human sense. At certain moments in the novel Eldritch exhibits a strange kinship with Barney and Leo. This kinship is made explicit as characters in the novel begin to manifest the stigmata of Eldritch. The characters reveal the presence of Eldritch within them: they are as much the children of Eldritch as they are the children of the transcendent form creator. As Barney explains to Anne, when she saw Barney manifest the stigmata of Eldritch, she was "seeing into absolute reality. The essence beyond the mere appearance" (219). The horror of Eldritch—and alien or god or demiurge Eldritch—is that his desire to spread himself through the solar system through Chew-Z is a reverse of the Christian redemption story. Instead of "God dying for man,"

Barney Mayerson notes, the characters were faced with a "superior power asking us to perish for *it*" (218).

What, exactly, does Chew-Z do? It traps its users in an isolated world where everything is a projection of the mind of Eldritch. It is a retreat into a peculiar kind of solipsism and, as such, a complete removal from the shared world of communal experience. It is an *anticommunion* element—a wafer that brings its users into communion with a type of antigod. In the typical gyrations of a Dick novel, however, one realizes that in coming into communion with Eldritch through the use of Chew-Z, one is at the same time rejecting the communal aspect of communion, for as each character begins to manifest the stigmata of Eldritch, it becomes evident that Eldritch is in fact a presence within everyone already. To say that under the influence of Chew-Z the landscape is a projection of Eldritch is to say that it is a projection of ourselves. We are Eldritch. As Barney begins to understand the true nature of Chew-Z, he notes that eventually Eldritch will "snare us all. Just like this. Isolated. The communal world is gone. At least for me; he began with me" (179). In a solipsistic environment, one's ability to act in empathy with a fellow human is removed: no authentic empathic connection can be made, for there is no authentic *other* one can achieve a communal experience with. The stigmata symbolize this: one cannot act in empathy with a fellow human with artificial eyes, teeth, and arm. One cannot have an authentically *human* experience with the cold and mechanical. At the end of the novel Leo comes to understand that the three stigmata of Eldritch represent the "evil, negative trinity of alienation, blurred reality, and despair" (229). In the world of Philip K. Dick, to lose the communal shared world—a world of empathy with one's fellow humans— is to become alienated from society, to live within an unstable reality, and to risk descent into utter despair. It is to take up residence in the tomb world. As Richard Hnatt notes after receiving his first evolutionary leap forward through E Therapy: "Below lay the tomb world, the immutable cause-and-effect world of the demonic. At median extended the layer of the human, but at any instant a man could plunge—descend as if sinking—into the hell-layer beneath. Or: he could ascend to the ethereal world above, which constituted the third of the trinary layers." The descent took the form of "Depression, all mental illness"—but the ascension was achieved "through empathy" (71).

The last word of the novel is not found at the end of the last chapter; it is found in the epigraph to the novel, which purports to be an excerpt from an audio-memo dictated by Leo Bulero upon his return to Earth: "I mean, after all; you have to consider we're only made out of dust. That's admittedly not much to go on and we shouldn't forget that. But even considering, I mean it's a sort of bad beginning, we're not doing too bad. So I personally have faith that even in this lousy situation we're faced with we can make it. You get me?" It is a moment—however slight—of hope in a novel where the triune threats of alienation, blurred reality, and despair are everywhere evident.

Flow My Tears, the Policeman Said

Flow My Tears, the Policeman Said is a novel filled with the pain of betrayal and lost love.[21] It is also filled with the wonder and mystery of human relationships. Dick often wrote about the breakdown of relationships—to be sure, it is difficult to name a Dick novel that does not deal in some fashion with a breaking or broken marriage—and *Flow My Tears* follows this pattern, but few other works (*The Transmigration of Timothy Archer* is one possible exception) deal so directly and forcefully with the psychological complexities of human heartbreak. The novel is a virtual catalog of human erotic contact: heterosexuality, homosexuality, lesbianism, incest, pedophilia, fetishism, sadomasochism, and even mass orgies conducted over a Dickean version of the Internet—all of these forms of human contact make an appearance in the novel. Coupled with these physical manifestations of desire, the novel features characters torn—even psychotically damaged—by the loneliness, rage, and grief that follow in the wake of lost love, of lost human contact. There are few moments of romance in the novel, and the psychological peace and security that accompany healthy human love (whether between lovers, between friends, or even between parent and child) is notably absent among the central characters of the narrative. The novel was drafted in an emotionally painful period of Dick's life (his fourth wife, Nancy, had left him, taking their child), and Dick poured the full measure of his grief into the novel.[22]

As discussed in relation to *Now Wait for Last Year,* Dick's novels are often vulnerable to the charge of logical inconsistency, and *Flow My Tears, the Policeman Said* is one of the more blatant offenders: there are simply too many inexplicable moments in the novel to casually explain away or overlook. Yet for all of this it remains one of the more significant works in the Dick canon and stands beside *The Man in the High Castle* as the only other of Dick's novels to receive a major award (the John W. Campbell Award for best science fiction novel of 1974). The key portrait in the novel is of the policeman of the work's title, Felix Buchman, whose complex relationship with his twin sister, Alys, who is also his wife and with whom he has had a child, is the key relationship in the novel. Alys, much to Felix's chagrin, is a drug abuser and sexual fetishist, but her death from an overdose of the time- and space-altering drug KR-3 sends Felix into a long and troubling paroxysm of despair.

The enemy of love is betrayal, and the novel is filled with characters who have become the desperate victims of betrayal. In the novel's opening scene, Jason Taverner is attacked by Marilyn Mason. Marilyn had been betrayed by Jason, who, when taking advantage of Marilyn, was betraying Heather Hart, who was having an affair with Alys Buchman, and so it goes from character to character throughout the novel. One of the first characters whom Jason Taverner meets after waking up sans identification in a seedy hotel is the document forger and police informant Kathy Nelson. Kathy has been driven psychotic through police blackmail and the pain of separation from her lover, Jack. Living in a "betrayal state," Kathy's seeming refusal to betray Jason to the authorities is almost inexplicable: Jason observes that "betrayal was an everyday event; a refusal to betray, as in his case, was miraculous" (70).[23]

The antidote to betrayal is empathy, and the two key interpretive scenes in *Flow My Tears* both deal with the psychological complexities of extending empathy. The first of these moments occurs in the middle of the novel when Ruth Rae relates to Jason Taverner the tale of the rabbit. Ruth tells of a pet rabbit whose great desire in life was to connect with the other household pets, particularly the cats. Although it did not have the inherent aptitudes of the cats, the rabbit strove to engage the cats in games—to "be with them and play with them as an equal" (108). But one day a visiting German shepherd, who did not know the rules of the games that the rabbit would play with the cats, bit the rabbit, giving it a nonfatal but severe wound. The rabbit was hurt in his efforts to connect interpersonally with the other animals.

Ruth says:

> But what was so touching about him was his pushing against the limits of his—what would you say?—physiology? His limitations as a rabbit, trying to become a more evolved life form, like the cats. Wanting all the time to be with them and play with them as an equal. That's all there is to it, really. . . . But look at the aspirations of that rabbit and look at his failing. A little life trying. And all the time it was hopeless. But the rabbit didn't know that. Or maybe he did know and kept trying anyhow. But I think he didn't understand. He just wanted to do it so badly. It was his whole life, because he loved the cats. (108–9)

Within the context of *Flow My Tears,* this story of the rabbit acts as a kind of parable about the desperate necessity to love and be loved. The tragic love of the rabbit was rewarded with pain, with a deep wound inflicted by an animal who did not understand the nature of the rabbit's game. Love is like that—it is an urge to connect that so often leads to psychological wounds. "Then why is love so good?" Jason asks Ruth (109). Love, Ruth answers, is that which allows the individual to "overcome instinct. Instincts push us into fighting for survival. . . . Survival of ourselves at the expense of others" (110). But love—despite the pain, the loss, the grief that inevitably follow—takes one outside of the self and integrates one with another. More than anything else, Ruth points out, grief is the "most powerful emotion a man or child or animal can feel" and is a "good feeling" because grief "causes you to leave yourself," and "you can't feel grief unless you've had love before it—grief is the final outcome of love, because it's love lost" (111).

Ruth's interpretation of the parable of the rabbit gives interpretive context for the second key moment in the novel. At the end of the novel, having lost his twin sister and bride, Alys, Felix Buchman weeps. Their relationship—beyond even the incestual controversy—was complicated: Felix strived for rule and order in life, and Alys was the very principle of disorder writ large. Felix sees himself as "fighting for a coherent society." He wants to "create order, structure, harmony," and this is why Alys "threatens" him, for she brings discord into his life (102). Yet Felix loves Alys, and her death sends him into a profound despair. In order to try to prevent the illicit nature of his relationship with Alys to become public after her death, Felix elects to frame Jason for the murder of Alys, a decision he rationalizes through the belief that his role in society is greater than Jason's, thus his life is worth preserving. Following this decision, Felix has a dream in which solemn and noble knights on horseback—led by an old king—march past Felix to a house where they execute Jason: "Within himself Felix Buchman felt absolute and utter desolate grief. But in the dream he did not go back nor look back. There was nothing that could be done. No one could have stopped the posse of varicolored men in robes; they could not have been said no to. Anyhow, it was over, Taverner was dead" (220). Felix wakes from this dream and goes to a gas station, where he meets a stranger, a middle-aged black man, and hands the stranger a piece of paper with a heart drawn on it. Felix turns to leave, but then, weeping once more, returns and hugs the stranger. The stranger does not push Felix away: it is a moment of empathy in which two strangers break through the conventions of polite society and connect. It is a moment of understanding born out of *philos*—a love born out of friendship and brotherhood. The purity of this empathic connection is overpowering. It is transformative. When Felix parts from the stranger, he resolves to go to Florida and bring his child home.

Love of a child, Felix had claimed earlier in the novel, is "the strongest form of love" (136). Felix is now ready to embrace those words in his own life.

As is true in so many of Dick's works, the power of humans to combat the forces of entropy and decay is limited. Often, the best individuals can achieve are small moments of creativity or of repair that give form back to the formless and thus, in their own small way, serve as a counter to the relentless efforts of entropy, the form destroyer. Pottery and pot-healing are key symbols for Dick in this regard, as noted earlier. True to form, the one character in *Flow My Tears* who represents a simple and honest approach to human connection is the pot-maker Mary Anne Dominic. At the end of the novel, a pot crafted by Mary becomes the symbol for the kind of love—simple, uncluttered by self-interest and ego—that can give form and shape to human interaction. Dick writes: the "blue vase made by Mary Anne Dominic and purchased by Jason Taverner as a gift for Heather Hart wound up in a private collection of modern pottery. It remains there to this day, and is much treasured. And, in fact, by a number of people who know ceramics, openly and genuinely cherished. And loved" (231).[24]

VALIS

Dick's life is as interesting as any of his novels, and in the alchemy of the Bay Area in the 1960s, Dick's life produced more than enough anecdotes to satisfy the needs of any modern celebrity gossip column. Yet his drug use, his multiple failed marriages, his struggles with poverty and paranoia, his childhood traumas, and his adult terrors all pale in comparison with the events of February and March 1974. The events of these two months defy easy summation; Dick himself would have trouble at times recounting the events in linear fashion.[25] But it seems to have started when Dick, suffering a toothache, had some pain medication delivered to his home. When he opened the door to receive the delivery, he was met by a young woman wearing a pendant of the Christian fish symbol around her neck. As he looked at the symbol, light from the sun was reflected off of it into Dick's eyes. For the next two months Dick was in a mystical fugue state, and for the remainder of the year Dick experienced intermittent visions and other uncanny events. He suddenly knew Latin and Greek phrases. He heard messages interwoven in Beatles records. It was revealed to him—through a moment of mystic awareness—that his son, Christopher, was endangered by an undiagnosed inguinal hernia (it was true, and Christopher was operated on in October 1974). He became aware of another being living inside of him—a persona Dick identified differently at different times, but most often as Thomas. He realized that time had actually stopped moving forward in A.D. 70 and did not resume again until 1945—concurrent with the discovery of the Gnostic Nag Hammadi scriptures.[26]

Dick would spend the rest of his life trying to come to terms with the revelations of that year. For the next several years he poured his energies into his *Exegesis,* his massive, sprawling journal, much of which is devoted to exploring a host of different interpretations of the events of 2–3–74 (as he came to refer to them), including what he called the "minimum hypothesis," which was that the whole thing was the by-product of a mind warped by drugs or psychosis.[27] Each of Dick's final four novels—*Radio Free Albemuth, VALIS, The Divine Invasion,* and *The Transmigration of Timothy Archer*—can be said, to one degree or another, to be the products of Dick's preoccupations in the *Exegesis.* But *VALIS* stands out from the other works in that it is a barely fictionalized rendering of the events of 1974. The first eight chapters of *VALIS* recount Dick's experiences in that year, and it is only with the introduction of the movie called *Valis* in chapter 9 that the novel heads into the realm of pure fiction. Readers of the *Exegesis* find Dick exploring countless theories in an attempt to explain to himself the mysteries of 1974, and although certain key themes are highlighted in the work, no coherent cosmological system emerges from the pages of the massive tome. What one finds in *VALIS* is *one* cosmological system derived by Dick in his quest to explain 2–3–74. It is, however, built on some of the central themes Dick returns to in myriad ways in the *Exegesis.* The cosmology of Horselover Fat (Dick's alter ego in *VALIS*) is distilled in the *Tractates: Cryptica Scriptura* distributed throughout the novel and collected in an appendix at the end of the narrative.[28] These *Tractates* are not lifted directly from the *Exegesis,* but were written by Dick specifically for *VALIS;* yet they do reflect much of Dick's metaphysical speculation in the *Exegesis,* and many of the concepts and terms in *Tractates* are derived from passages in the larger work.[29] By splitting "himself" into two characters (who are really one character) in *VALIS*—Horselover Fat and Phil Dick— Dick is able to serve as his own commentator, and thus the reader is given both cosmology and commentary at the same time. As Phil Dick, the narrator of *VALIS,* notes, "I am Horselover Fat, and I am writing this in the third person to gain much-needed objectivity" (11).[30]

Dick's cosmology presented in *VALIS* is rooted in Gnosticism, but it is a Gnosticism that is infused with Platonic idealism, Zoroastrianism, Christianity, pre-Socratic philosophy, Jungian psychoanalytic theory, and a blend of other theological systems Dick had ingested in his quest to solve the riddles of 1974. Dick's cosmology—or, more properly, Horselover Fat's cosmology—in *VALIS* is based on the "Two Source Cosmogony" presented in *Tractate* #47.[31] In the beginning there was the One (the ultimate transcendent God). In this ultimate being all things were contained. In order to separate the "was not" from the "was" in itself (that is, to separate the light from the dark, the yin and the yang), the One created an egg that contained complementary twins. Upon full gestation, these twins would emerge and through their intermingling give rise to the universe with all of its objects and forms. One of the pair (Form II), however, in its eagerness to exist, broke out of the shell prematurely and, as a result, was not properly formed. The other of the pair (Form I) remained until it was fully formed, and thus was born without defect. Each of these beings gave rise to a "hyperuniverse": Form I gave rise to Hyperuniverse I; Form II gave rise to Hyperuniverse II. Through the interconnection of these two hyperuniverses, the "hologramatic" universe in which humans exist came into being. The goal of this intermingling was to bring about the creation of beings that would evolve until they became "isomorphic" with the One (that is to say, they would be similar in form and structure to the One, although they would also be genetically different from the One).

The problem with the plan is that the defects in Form II were transferred into Hyperuniverse II, and subsequently into the holographic universe of human sensory experience. As products of this holographic universe, therefore, humans are damaged—they carry with them (in type if not if in actuality) the wounds of the prematurely born Form II. This has impaired the "teaching" function of the holographic universe, which has inhibited humans from becoming isomorphic with the One. From the damaged nature of Form II, suffering, disorder, evil, and entropy have entered the holographic universe. And thus Dick presents a version of the Gnostic response to the theodicy problem.

The holographic universe is created by the layering of two hyperuniverses, and thus "reality" as humans experience it is layered. One layer—that emanating from Form II—is the realm of entropy and decay and deterministic laws, and it is called the Black Iron Prison, or the Empire. The other realm, from Form I, is the Palm Tree Garden. The Palm Tree Garden is hidden from most humans, for they suffer the damage of Form II. To become enlightened is to see the Black Iron Prison for what it is, and to gain a vision of the Palm Tree Garden. The mechanism of enlightenment is anamnesis—a concept arising out of Plato—in which one loses the amnesia of spiritual occlusion and "remembers" the true nature of the holographic universe and understands the true relationship between it and the One.

In order to help humans overcome the blindness and defects generated in them by Form II, Form I sent a "micro-form" of itself into the holographic universe in order to heal human spiritual wounds. This is the savior, as fulfilled in the person of Jesus Christ (as well as the Buddha). The deranged Form II, however, unaware of its own deformed nature, viewed the "micro-form" of Form I as a type of invader and killed it. Subsequently Form I seeks to destroy Form II in order to separate the commingled hyperuniverses and restore the original teaching function to the holographic universe.

The universe is composed of information. Knowledge of the true nature of the universe comes in the form of gnosis—an influx of knowledge, of information. The savior is called a Plasmate (as in the plasma of Christ, the blood of Christ in the communion grail). The Plasmate can fuse itself with a human, creating a homoplasmate. To the homoplasmate is available knowledge of the One and of the true nature and purpose of creation. The saving gnosis is that which provides humans with the ability, through anamnesis, to shed the blindness inherited from Form II, to break through the walls of the Black Iron Prison, and to see clearly—through remembered knowledge—the One and to become isomorphic with it. Until such enlightenment comes, the Palm Tree Garden and the One are hidden from human view. But through the work of the Plasmate, an element of rationality had broken into the irrational world and was slowly transforming it. This rational element is often hidden from view—it is disguised amid the irrationality of the Black Iron Prison. It blends into its cosmic landscape the way the stripes of the Zebra provided a natural, blended camouflage. This is the Zebra Principle, and in *VALIS*, Phil/Fat uses *Zebra* as a kind of intellectual shorthand for God—the One.[32] As Phil Dick, the narrator, describes it in *VALIS:*

> The universe might be irrational, but something rational had broken into it, like a thief in the night breaks into a sleeping household, unexpectedly in terms of place, in terms of time. Fat had seen it—not because there was anything special about him—but because it had wanted him to see it.
>
> Normally it remained camouflaged. Normally when it appeared no one could distinguish it from ground—set to ground, as Fat correctly expressed it. He had a name for it.
>
> Zebra. Because it blended. The name for this is mimesis. Another name is mimicry. . . .
>
> What if a high form of sentient mimicry existed—such a high form that no human (or few humans) had detected it? What if it could only be detected if it *wanted* to be detected? (69)

A detection of a higher order of being—of a god—whose presence in the empirical world (the world of the Black Iron Prison) is masked through mimicry would require a special infilling knowledge, a theophany, which would open closed doors of perception.

To read *VALIS* is to read a thinly fictionalized account of Dick's own quest for gnosis—for a theophany or epiphany that would explain satisfactorily the events of 2–3–74. The experiences of Horselover Fat are—in many cases—the experiences of Philip K. Dick, at least through the first eight chapters. In the remaining chapters of the novel, the lives of Philip K. Dick and Phil/Fat diverge. The trek to meet Eric and Linda Lampton and then his meeting Sophia—the two-year-old who may be the reborn savior, a new incarnation of divine wisdom in the holographic universe—followed by the psychic healing of Phil/Fat, are a fictional rendering of the literalized implications of the "two source cosmogony." Phil/Fat's quest for gnosis does not end with his meeting Sophia, unfortunately. The accidental killing of the child triggers a redivision of Phil's psyche back into Phil/Fat, and the book ends with both halves of the psyche searching—each in its different way—for the next coming of the savior.

Conclusion
Apologia pro mea vita

No one novel or story can be said to capture the essence of Philip K. Dick.[1] In fact Dick is an author best appreciated through reading widely through his canon. Despite the fact that certain individual works by Dick are true masterpieces of the science fiction genre and stand out from the pack accordingly, the collective impact of his works produces something Dick himself found intriguing as a concept, and one that he discussed in numerous works: a gestalt. Dick's career is, in a certain sense, greater than the sum of its parts. His themes—entropy, repair, epistemology, paranoia, the nature of self-identity, of humanity, of reality—bind his works together, and reading deeply in his canon gives one a sense of the way these themes evolve from one work to the next and from one decade of his career to the next.

During the three decades of his writing career, Dick explored numerous philosophical, theological, sociological, and political ideas. He did not often have answers to the questions he raised, but he was relentless with his questions. Although no one idea or theme of Dick's can be said to contain the rest—the works are too diverse for that—there is one idea that Dick returned to with such frequency, and which many of his other themes were made to serve in countless different ways, that one can say it was the dominant theme of his career. Stated as a question, Dick asked throughout his career if one can ever know—know, in terms Descartes might appreciate, with absolute certainty—the *absolute*. Behind the thin fabric of human civilization saturated with power politics, technology, and media, above both broken and successful human relationships, beyond the epistemological problems caused by human subjectivity, *what is there?* Is *it* knowable?

In 1967, in the middle of his career, Dick published one of his greatest short stories, "The Electric Ant." In this tale the main character, Garson Poole, as a result of an accident that severs one of his hands, discovers that, much to his surprise, he is not human: he is an "electric ant," an organic robot. Soon afterward Poole discovers that reality, as he perceives it, is a construct fed to him through a slow-moving programming tape in his chest. By manipulating the tape, he can manipulate his perception of reality. What would happen, Poole asks himself, if he were to remove the tape entirely? He would feel all things at once. The knowledge of the universe itself would be, once and for all, made known to him. "What I want," Poole realizes, "is ultimate and absolute reality, for one microsecond. After that it doesn't matter, because all will be known; nothing will be left to understand or see."[2]

In his introduction to a reprint edition of *Solar Lottery* in 1976, science fiction author and critic Thomas M. Disch wrote: "Dick's major theme, the one that consistently calls forth his finest and most forceful work, is transcendence—whether it's possible, what it feels like, and whether that feeling ultimately represents wishful thinking or some larger reality. He is constantly torn between a rationalistic denial of the ultimate reality of transcendent experience and a (still ironic) celebration of the brute fact of it" (Disch 23). Like the romantics of the early nineteenth century, Dick yearned for transcendence, for direct contact with the transcendent, and there were moments in his life when he believed he did indeed bridge the gap between the human and the transcendent, between humans and God. So strange were many of these events, and they avoided explanation so completely, that Dick was torn between belief and doubt, and even though he had the evidence of his own experience to validate belief, he left room for skepticism and acknowledged—on occasion—that his own mystical experiences could be nothing more than the hallucinations of an unstable mind.

Dick's works are about characters who will go to any length to encounter the transcendent and who, having met the transcendent face to face (in whatever guise), will go to any length to try to understand the nature of the encounter. These are no easy tasks. In a world in which *reality* is a fluid concept and self-identity is constantly in flux, discovering and coming to terms with transcendent forces—godlike, *supra*rational, forces, be they good or evil—rivals the greatest of philosophical questions. The "gods" of Dick's works are simultaneously revealed and hidden from his characters. They are good, and they are evil. They are direct and present, and they are strange and foreign. Encounters with these transcendent forces coerce his characters to ask about the nature of reality and the nature of the self, about the nature of good and evil, about warfare, and about human kindness. Of all of the ideas that this novelist of ideas struggled with, coming to terms with the relationship between the human and the transcendent was chief among them, and it is this theme that incorporates the rest and gives shape and significance to the life and the work of Philip K. Dick.

Notes

Chapter 1—Understanding Philip K. Dick

1. The interview can be found in Rickman, *Philip K. Dick: The Last Testament,* 22–23.

2. For treatments of Dick's biography, see Sutin's *Divine Invasions* and Rickman's *To the High Castle,* as well as the chronologies and biographical sketches available in Mackey, *Philip K. Dick;* Robinson, *Novels of Philip K. Dick;* Warrick, *Mind in Motion;* and Williams, *Only Apparently Real.* The Williams study, as well as Rickman's *Philip K. Dick: In His Own Words* and *Philip K. Dick: The Last Testament,* contain transcriptions of numerous extended interviews with Dick, and thus are valuable sources for biographical material. Anne Dick's *Search for Philip K. Dick* and Carrère's *I Am Alive and You Are Dead* are additional resources for biographical information, but should be approached with some caution. The biographical details used in this study are gathered from the studies by Sutin, Rickman, Williams, Robinson, Mackey, and Warrick.

3. For more on this encounter with the FBI recruiters, see Sutin, *Divine Invasions,* 83–84.

Chapter 2—Philip K. Dick, Novelist of Ideas

1. Some evidence suggests that *Nicholas and the Higs* may have had a few science fiction elements, but it was marketed as a mainstream work.

2. For more discussion of the realist novels, see Robinson, *Novels of Philip K. Dick,* 1–12, 20–23; and Mackey, *Philip K. Dick,* 31–46. Brief summaries of the realist novels can be found in Butler, *Philip K. Dick;* for a general discussion of the history and relative merits of these works, see the roundtable discussion moderated by David G. Hartwell, "Philip K. Dick: The Mainstream Novels," *New York Review of Science Fiction* 7 (October 1994), 12–18. As opposed to

the negative critique of the realist novels found in Robinson, the panelists in the Hartwell roundtable are much more enthusiastic in their assessment.

3. Robinson characterizes the main subject of the mainstream novels in this manner: they are about "the effect, in American postwar capitalism, of business relations on the personal relations between employer and employee, and indirectly on all personal relations. Dick believed this effect to be profoundly destructive. This belief lies at the center of most of these realist novels, and the destruction of human relations by business relations may be said to be their subject" (*Novels of Philip K. Dick,* 3).

4. See Rickman, *Philip K. Dick: In His Own Words,* 133.

5. For some general and definitional treatments of science fiction, consult: Aldiss and Wingrove, *Trillion Year Spree;* Roberts, *Science Fiction;* Clareson, *Understanding Contemporary American Science Fiction;* Harris-Fain, *Understanding Contemporary American Science Fiction;* Landon, *Science Fiction after 1900;* James and Mendlesohn, *Cambridge Companion to Science Fiction;* James Gunn and Matthew Candelaria, eds., *Speculations on Speculation: Theories of Science Fiction* (Lanham, Md.: Scarecrow Press, 2005).

6. Darko Suvin, "Estrangement and Cognition," reprinted in Gunn and Candelaria, *Speculations on Speculation,* 23–35; see 27 for the quoted material.

7. See Dick's forward to *The Preserving Machine,* in Mullen et al., *On Philip K. Dick,* 16.

8. Dick, *Shifting Realities,* 99.

9. See Dick, *Shifting Realities,* 76.

10. See Dick, *Shifting Realities,* 75.

11. See Dick, *Shifting Realities,* 75. Dick's discussion of the blended nature of science fiction here bears strong resemblance to the nineteenth-century concept of the modern romance, with its transgeneric blending of the real and unreal, the realistic and the fantastic. For an extended treatment of the concept of the modern romance in nineteenth-century American literature, see G. R. Thompson and Eric

Carl Link, *Neutral Ground: New Traditionalism and the American Romance Controversy* (Baton Rouge: Louisiana State University Press, 1999).

12. Dick, *Shifting Realities*, 75.

13. Dick, from the essay "Pessimism in Science Fiction" (1955), reprinted in *Shifting Realities*, 54.

14. Dick, *Shifting Realities*, 54.

15. Dick, *Shifting Realities*, 63.

16. For a few studies of the relationship between science fiction and postmodernism, see: Hollinger "Science Fiction and Postmodernism"; M. Keith Booker, *Monsters, Mushroom Clouds, and the Cold War: American Science Fiction and the Roots of Postmodernism* (Westport, Conn.: Greenwood, 2001); Jorge Martins Rosa, "A Misreading Gone Too Far? Baudrillard Meets Philip K. Dick," *Science Fiction Studies* 35.1 (March 2008): 60–71; Butler, "Science Fiction as Postmodernism" See also see the special issue "Science Fiction and Postmodernism," *Science Fiction Studies* 18.3 (1991), especially the often-discussed essays by Jean Baudrillard. For a full-length study of Dick in the context of postmodernism, see Palmer, *Philip K. Dick*.

17. For instance, critic Csicsery-Roney writes the following about the connection between Dick's work and postmodernism: "Dick has also been the most influential catalyst in shifting SF theorists from earlier critical categories derived from traditional modernism to the categories of postmodernism. Dick's themes, it turned out, were not just the wild 'what ifs' of SF; they were the guiding ideas of postmodern culture. The alternate history, which in Dick's hands questions the possibility of any authentic history, is cognate with the Foucauldian critique of Grand History. The fascination with disintegrating realities is cognate with the rise of the theory of schizophrenia as a cultural dominant in the late 20th century (developed in the works of R. D. Laing, Joseph Gabel, Deleuze and Guattari, Gregory Bateson, and many other theorists who arrived at the idea independently of one another) and of deconstructions of substantive rationality. The

notion of the artificial, technologically induced manipulation of the fundamental experience of reality is cognate with the idea of virtual reality and with simulation theory. The problem of androids and homeostatic mechanisms, which leads to such rich ambivalence in Dick's fiction, has emerged as a full-fledged science-fictional philosophical model in the political theory of cyborgs" (in Mullen et al., *On Philip K. Dick,* vi).

18. Palmer, *Philip K. Dick,* 4.

19. See Baudrillard's essay "Simulacra and Science Fiction," *Science Fiction Studies* 18.3 (1991): 309–13.

20. On the pervasive use of "simulation" in Dick's works, see Rossi, "Fourfold Symmetry," 399–400. There is a connection between postmodernist concepts of simulacra and poststructuralist language theory, and a case can be—and has been—made that Dick has explored this connection, highlighting the breakdown of the relationship between the sign and the signified in ways that illustrate the erasure of the logos itself. See Christopher Palmer's discussion of this notion in Dick's *Time Out of Joint* in "Philip K. Dick," 395.

21. See Frederic Jameson, *Postmodernism, or The Cultural Logic of Late Capitalism* (Durham, N.C.: Duke University Press, 1991).

22. For a discussion of Dick as a pioneer in creating "meta-SF," see Malmgren, "Meta-SF."

23. Landon, *Science Fiction after 1900,* 113.

24. Landon writes: "Even more explicitly, his *The Man in the High Castle* implicates art in the construction of reality, featuring a novel-within-the-novel that presents a history much closer to our own than the alternate history of the frame novel, while also offering a detailed investigation of aesthetics. As Dick has explained, one of his purposes in writing such a fiction was to show how the subjective world of one powerful person can infringe on the world of another person, thus exerting the greatest power one human being can exert over others. Of course, this 'greatest power one human can exert over others' is precisely the power of effective novelists whose literary semblances momentarily displace the referential reality of their readers" (*Science Fiction after 1900,* 113–14).

25. The concept of the illness story was developed by Richard Ohmann. See the discussion of Ohmann's concept and its relationship to American fiction of the 1960s and 1970s in Raymond Mazurek, "Courses and Canons: The Post-1945 U.S. Novel," *Critique* 31.3 (Spring 1990): 143–56.

26. Ohmann, as summarized in Mazurek, "Courses and Canons," 146.

27. From "If You Find This World Bad, You Should See Some of the Others," an address Dick delivered in Metz, France, at a science fiction convention in 1977. The address is reprinted in *Shifting Realities*. See 234 for the quote.

28. Dick, "Mainstream That through the Ghetto Flows," 164.

29. Palmer, "Philip K. Dick," 392.

30. Or as Istvan Csicsery-Ronay Jr. has written in his review entitled "The Wife's Story," Dick's method employs a "double operation of the imagination—making the everyday the scene of metaphysical conflict, and then making the metaphysical prosaic" (*Science Fiction Studies* 24.2 [July 1997]: 326)

31. Stanislaw Lem, "Science Fiction: A Hopeless Case—With Exceptions," 81, reprinted in Gillespie, *Philip K. Dick,* 69–94.

Chapter 3—The Craft and Career of Philip K. Dick

1. In *Only Apparently Real* (145), Paul Williams divides Dick's career into three main stages: the beginnings to the composition of *Humpty Dumpty in Oakland* (1951–60); the *Man in the High Castle* to the composition of *Flow My Tears, the Policeman Said* (1961–70); and Dick's "The Android and the Human" address to the composition of *The Transmigration of Timothy Archer* (1972–81). Meanwhile, Gregg Rickman, in *Philip K. Dick: In His Own Words* (13–16), offers a four-stage career: (1) 1952–60; (2) 1962–65 (from *High Castle* through *Dr. Bloodmoney*); (3) 1966–76 (from *Counter-Clock World* through *Flow My Tears*); and (4) 1977–81 (from *A Scanner Darkly* until the end of Dick's career). Darko Suvin offered a three-stage career in 1975, prior to the publication of *A Scanner Darkly*. In Suvin's early assessment, Dick's career can be traced

through three stages: from the beginnings through *High Castle* (viewing *High Castle* as the culmination of an apprenticeship period rather than the genesis of a new stage), from *High Castle* to *The Three Stigmata of Palmer Eldritch* (1962–65), and from 1966 through *Ubik* (1969) (Suvin, "Artifice as Refuge," 73).

2. See Robinson, *Novels of Philip K. Dick,* 13–15.

3. Dick, as quoted in Rickman, *Philip K. Dick: In His Own Words,* 116.

4. All page references are to *The Cosmic Puppets* (New York: Vintage, 2003) This reference to Armaiti's dark locks makes her one of Dick's first "dark-haired women." See the discussion of Dick's female characters later in this chapter.

5. Much of this paragraph, excluding the particulars of plot, could also be said of Dick's ambitious but flawed potboiler *The Game-Players of Titan* (w. 1963, p. 1963).

6. All page references are to *Solar Lottery* (New York: Vintage, 2003).

7. For additional introductions to Dick's science fiction in the 1950s, see Mackey, *Philip K. Dick,* chapter 2; and Robinson, *Novels of Philip K. Dick,* chapter 2.

8. Dick discussed some of this shift from his early pulp work to his later work in a 1977 essay, where he wrote that his earlier stories "were written when my life was simpler and made sense. I could tell the difference between the real world and the world I wrote about. . . . Later, when my personal life became complicated and full of unfortunate convolutions . . . I became educated to the fact that the greatest pain does not come zooming down from a distant planet, but up from the depths of the heart. Of course, both could happen; your wife and child could leave you, and you could be sitting alone in your empty house with nothing to live for, and in addition the Martians could bore through the roof to get you" (Dick, as quoted in Sutin, *Divine Invasions,* 74).

9. As one critic noted: "Dick provided a transition between the social satire fore-grounded in 1950s SF such as Pohl's and

Kornbluth's *The Space Merchants* and the almost exclusively interior-focused writing of the New Wave" (Landon, *Science Fiction after 1900,* 112).

10. The term *New Wave* was borrowed by literary critics from French film critics of the 1960s, who used the term to describe certain trends—established by directors such as Jean-Luc Godard and Francois Truffaut—of experimental cinema.

11. Gillespie, *Philip K. Dick,* 9–11.

12. For a discussion of Dick's "multifoci" point of view, see Robinson, *Novels of Philip K. Dick,* 5+; Suvin, "Artifice as Refuge"; and Rickman, *Philip K. Dick: In His Own Words,* 84–87.

13. About the female character types, Robinson writes: "Dick has said that he modeled his female characters on the two main characters from Thackeray's *Vanity Fair:* Becky Sharp and Amelia. The Becky Sharps are ambitious, manipulative, attractive, and dangerous to the men who are attracted to them. The Amelias are passive, weak, clinging: they tend to be wives who complain to, but never help, their husbands" (*Novels of Philip K. Dick,* 5). We meet these two types over and over again in Dick's work.

14. See Sutin, *Divine Invasions,* 109, for discussion.

15. There have been nonbiographical explanations as well: see, for instance, Mackey, *Philip K. Dick,* 108–9, who reads Dick's seeming hostility toward women as a symbolic representation of a Jungian anima.

16. For a treatment of Dick's characters in terms of gender theory, see Holliday, "Masculinity in the Novels of Philip K. Dick."

17. From his forward to *The Preserving Machine,* reprinted in Mullen et al., *On Philip K. Dick,* 16. For more on Dick's narrative strategies, see Sutin, *Divine Invasions,* 75–76, for a discussion of the "inner projection story"—in which "internal psychological contents were projected onto the outer world and became three-dimensional and real and concrete" (Dick, as quoted in Sutin, *Divine Invasions*); and Sutin, *Divine Invasions,* 136–39, for an overview of Dick's formula for plot development.

18. See Lee and Sauter, 135. See Sutin's treatment of the friendship of Bishop Pike and Philip K. Dick in *Divine Invasions,* 149–51.

19. See Lee and Sauter, 63.

20. In one interview, Dick said of *Transmigration,* "It's about a bishop who becomes intoxicated with the fervor of religious zeal. And it leads him to madness and death" (Dick, as quoted in Rickman, *Philip K. Dick: In His Own Words,* 203). For more on *Transmigration,* see Warrick, *Mind in Motion,* chapter 9; Robinson, *Novels of Philip K. Dick,* 120–25; and Mackey, *Philip K. Dick,* 124–27.

Chapter 4—The Themes of Philip K. Dick

1. Dick was not shy about either receiving external critique of his works or engaging in self-analysis. In fact he seemed to thrive on both—even when he, at times, vehemently disagreed with a particular critical comment here and there. As is clear from his own commentary on his works, Dick was aware that many of his works dealt with two major themes: what is real? and what is human? In the body of criticism that has sprung up around Dick's life and works, certain other related themes have been identified and are treated regularly in assessments of Dick's work. Many critics, for instance, have discussed the role of paranoia in Dick's work and the role of the "little man" or repairman as a defender of order against the universal forces of entropy. These were preoccupations of Dick's from his earliest stories through his final efforts. In her study of Dick's major works, Patricia Warrick (*Mind in Motion*) identifies eight central themes in Dick's works: power struggles, madness, apocalyptic destruction, the nature of good and evil, the question of what defines the human, the forces of entropy and death, drugs, and the quest for God. Another useful overview of Dick's principal themes is presented by Rickman in *Philip K. Dick: In His Own Words.* Rickman discusses, among other items, Dick's use of a variety of compelling binary oppositions in his works, such as good versus evil, entropy versus repair, human versus android, caritas versus heartlessness, and so forth (see, in particular, chapter 2 of Rickman's study). This

present study owes much to these previous treatments of theme, as well as the body of Dick criticism generally.

2. For more discussion of this topic, see Fitting, "Reality as Ideological Construct"; for a discussion of cybernetic themes—especially those with implications for information theory and the mutually affecting relationship between the subject and the object in cybernetics, see Hayles, "Schizoid Android" Dick was clearly interested in cybernetics and discussed the field in his 1972 address "The Android and the Human"—see Dick, *Shifting Realities*, 183–84.

3. Dick would later reflect back on "Roog" in this manner: In "Roog" can be found "the basis of much of my twenty-seven years of professional writing: the attempt to get into another person's head, or another creature's head, and see out from his eyes or its eyes, and the more different that person is from the rest of us the better. You start with the sentient entity and work outward, inferring its world. . . . I began to develop the idea that each creature lives in a world somewhat different from all the other creatures and their worlds" (*Collected Stories*, vol. 1, 402).

4. See Williams, *Only Apparently Real*, 169.

5. See Fitting's discussion of *Eye in the Sky* in "Reality as Ideological Construct." Dick once noted that in *Eye in the Sky*, "I tried to show that the construction of a normative reality was not simply a non-conflictual consensus of individual subjectivities. In that novel each of the four subjective worlds implied domination—the exclusive imposition of that structure on others—the result of which was that the ideal of American democracy as a consensual pluralism yielded to the combined interests of the arms industry and the state" (Dick, as quoted in Fitting, "Reality as Ideological Construct," 98).

6. See Sutin, *Divine Invasions*, 90.

7. See Rickman, *Philip K. Dick: In His Own Words*, 120–21.

8. The letter can be found in Gillespie, *Philip K. Dick*, 31–33.

9. Dick, as quoted in Williams, *Only Apparently Real*, 169–70.

10. See Dick, *Shifting Realities*, 218. Dick's interest in the *idios kosmos* and *koinos kosmos* paralleled his interest in Jungian psychology. Dick was a confirmed Jungian from the time of his brief enrollment

at Berkeley forward, and he believed in the reality of the collective unconscious. Jung gave Dick the psychological framework (through the concept of the collective unconsciousness) upon which he could build his perennial investigation of the *idios kosmos* and the *koinos kosmos* (see Rickman, *Philip K. Dick: The Last Testament*, 25; Williams, *Only Apparently Real*, 55–56; and Dick's letter to *SF Commentary* in Gillespie, *Philip K. Dick*, 32). Dick's interest in the discrepancies between the *idios kosmos* and *koinos kosmos* also helps to explain his use of the "multi-foci" point of view, for it allows him to explore the shifting nature of the *idios kosmos*—see Robinson's comments on this (*Novels of Philip K. Dick*, 15–17). Dick's beliefs about the nature of subjectivity and the development of the *idios kosmos* were in part derived from his reading of Immanuel Kant—see Dick's 1964 essay "Drugs, Hallucinations, and the Quest for Reality," reprinted in *Shifting Realities*, especially his comments on 171.

11. See Rickman, *Philip K. Dick: In His Own Words*, 128.

12. *Collected Stories*, vol. 2, 381.

13. About this idea, Dick wrote: "That's one of the few original ideas I've ever contributed to science fiction. I mean, most of my ideas are rehash—but that was my original idea, was that a guy could be an android and not know it" (Lee and Sauter 37). For a reading of "Imposter" within the context of poststructural renderings of the doppelgänger motif, see Easterbrook, "Dianoia/Paranoia."

14. See, for instance, Sutin, *Divine Invasions*, 18–19.

15. Dick, *Shifting Realities*, 211–12.

16. *Collected Stories*, vol. 2, 380.

17. For an extended treatment of the doppelgänger motif in *Do Androids Dream*, see Warrick, *Mind in Motion*, chapter 6.

18. The Voigt-Kampff test seems to operate on a principle similar to the Turing Test proposed by the mathematician and computer scientist Alan Turing in the 1950s. For more, see Andrew M. Butler, "Philip K. Dick, *Do Androids Dream of Electric Sheep?*" in *The Popular and the Canonical: Debating Twentieth-Century Literature 1940–2000*, ed. David Johnson (London: Routledge, 2005], 137.

19. All page references are to *Do Androids Dream of Electric Sheep?* (New York: Del Ray, 1996).

20. For more on Dick's treatment of the *human,* see Gillis, "Dick on the Human."

21. *Collected Stories,* vol. 3, 137.

22. Rickman, *Philip K. Dick: In His Own Words,* 46.

23. For some discussion of the biographical basis for Dick's interest in repair and repairmen, see Sutin, *Divine Invasions,* chapter 3. In Sutin's words, the "lovely, cranky figure of the 'repairman' also recurs as a symbol of integrity and courage in the face of impossible odds" (*Divine Invasions,* 53).

24. Gillespie, *Philip K. Dick,* 45.

25. Williams, as quoted in Rickman, *Philip K. Dick: In His Own Words,* 16–17.

26. Dick, in Gillespie, *Philip K. Dick,* 45.

27. All page references are to *Ubik* (New York: Vintage, 1991).

28. Dick, as quoted in Sutin, *Divine Invasions,* 200.

29. For a brief discussion of commodity fetishization as it relates to *Ubik,* see Roberts, *Science Fiction,* 148–51. Roberts makes a connection between this Marxist concept and the paranoia found in the "things" in a Dick novel (the talking doors make one's life miserable in *Ubik,* and so forth). See also Freedman's discussion of paranoia in *Ubik* in "Towards a Theory of Paranoia."

30. See, for instance, Williams, *Only Apparently Real,* 72, where Williams quotes Dick talking about *Ubik* in terms of Platonic philosophy. See also Warrick, *Mind in Motion,* 141.

31. For a discussion of the *Bardo Thodol* and its relationship to *Ubik,* see Pierce, *Philip K. Dick,* 30–31.

32. For a brief overview of some of the different interpretive responses to the ending, see Mackey, *Philip K. Dick,* 94.

33. All page references are to, *Galactic Pot-Healer* (New York: Vintage, 1994)

34. Faust's attempt to drain the swamp is analogous to Glimmung's attempt to raise Heldscalla from the sea, and so forth. See Dick, *Galactic Pot-Healer,* 89–91.

35. For discussion, see Warrick, *Mind in Motion,* 99; Robinson, *Novels of Philip K. Dick,* 101; Warren, "Search for Absolutes," 174–82; and Mackey, *Philip K. Dick,* 96–99.

36. Prior to joining Glimmung's efforts to raise Heldscalla, Joe spends his spare time playing "The Game." In this game, one takes a well-known title or phrase in English, feeds it through an automatic translation program in order to convert the phrase to a foreign language, then takes the translation and retranslates it back into English. Thus *Breakfast at Tiffany's* becomes "Quickly Shattered at the Quarreling Posterior" (9). The object of the game is to try to guess what the original phrase or title was. Even in this game, the human compulsion to combat the forces of entropy is evident: the original title has been subject to a type of linguistic decay, and the object of the person playing the game is to try to restore linguistic order to the degenerated translation.

37. Dick, as quoted in Williams, *Only Apparently Real,* 134–35.

38. See Sutin, *Divine Invasions,* 128.

39. There is considerable disagreement among religious scholars over just what constitutes a "Gnostic" religion. What is certainly true is that there is no *one* Gnosticism, but a number of different Gnostic systems. It would not be accurate, generally speaking, to call Dick a Gnostic (even though he did so himself on a couple of occasions). What would be more accurate is to note that Dick was interested in the Gnostic response to orthodox Christianity, and that in some of his explorations of the problem of pain and the nature of evil, he borrowed liberally from certain strains of Gnostic thought. For more on this topic, see McKee, *Pink Beams of Light,* especially 27–33; but see also DiTommaso, "Gnosticism and Dualism," for someone else's perspective.

40. This essay was an outgrowth of Dick's ongoing efforts throughout the 1970s to come to terms with his life, his writings, and, most important, his mystical experiences in early 1974. His outlet for this introspection was his vast journal, the *Exegesis.* In 1978 Dick sent "Cosmogony and Cosmology" to his agent, but it was not published until 1987 (see Dick, *Shifting Realities,* 166). This essay summarizes

some of the ideas that emerge in the *Exegesis,* and is reprinted in *Shifting Realities,* 281–313.

41. This theory has elements in common with theodicies emerging from what is called process theology.

42. *Collected Stories,* vol. 2, 150.

43. All page references are to *The Divine Invasion* (New York: Vintage, 1991).

44. Dick, as quoted in Lee and Sauter, 30.

45. Mackey, *Philip K. Dick,* 9–10.

46. For this reason, Dick's works have lent themselves to productive work by Marxist-leaning critics, who find in Dick countless examples of commodity fetishization. For a Marxist reading of paranoia in Dick's work—a reading building off of the notion of commodity fetishization—see Freedman, "Towards a Theory of Paranoia." Freedman sees one of Dick's great achievements to be "his uniquely rigorous and consistent representations of human subjects caught in the web of commodities and conspiracies" ("Towards a Theory of Paranoia," 13).

47. For discussion of the distinction between authenticity and inauthenticity in Dick's works, see the studies done by Christopher Palmer.

48. For a treatment of the interaction of the media and the conscious mind in Dick's works, see Enns, "Media, Drugs, and Schizophrenia." For treatments of Dick's works in the context of contemporary media and information theory, see Enns, "Media, Drugs, and Schizophrenia"; and Suvin, "Goodbye and Hello."

49. Dick, as quoted in Williams, *Only Apparently Real,* 157.

50. Dick, as quoted in Williams, *Only Apparently Real,* 159.

51. Dick, *Shifting Realities,* 208.

52. See Sutin, *Divine Invasions,* 43, where Dick is quoted discussing the awareness of the potential loss of the self and the fear that this awareness generates. See also Mackey's discussion of the paranoia of the 1950s and how it is reflected in Dick's short fiction from the period (*Philip K. Dick,* 7).

53. For more on *A Scanner Darkly* and its relationship to Dick's life in the late 1960s and early 1970s, see Warrick, *Mind in Motion,* chapter 8; Sutin, *Divine Invasions,* 201–5; and Mackey, *Philip K. Dick,* 109–11. For some of Dick's own thoughts on this period of his life, see Dick's letter reprinted in Gillespie, *Philip K. Dick,* 49–52. See also Youngquist, "Score, Scan, Schiz." For a look at the role drugs plays in Dick's examinations of media technology, see Enns, "Media, Drugs, and Schizophrenia"

54. Dick, "Mainstream That through the Ghetto Flows," 180.

Chapter 5—Reading Philip K. Dick: Notes on Six Novels

1. The Hugo Award—named after science fiction magazine pioneer Hugo Gernsback—is sponsored by the World Science Fiction Society and presented each year to the best science fiction novel as determined by vote at the annual World Science Fiction Convention. *The Man in the High Castle* won the Hugo at the 1963 convention.

2. Good introductions to *The Man in the High Castle* include Warrick, *Mind in Motion,* chapter 2; Mackey, *Philip K. Dick,* 47–52; Clareson, *Understanding Contemporary American Science Fiction,* 155–65; Pierce, *Philip K. Dick,* chapter 3; and Robinson, *Novels of Philip K. Dick,* chapter 4 Additional in-depth treatments of the novel of note include Palmer, *Philip K. Dick,* chapter 6; N. B. Hayles, "Metaphysics and Metafiction in *The Man in the High Castle,*" in Greenberg and Olander, *Philip K. Dick,* 53–71; Cassie Carter, "The Metacolonization of Dick's *The Man in the High Castle:* Mimicry, Parasitism, and Americanism in the PSA," *Science Fiction Studies* 22.3 (1995): 333–42; John Rieder, "The Metafictive World of *The Man in the High Castle,*" *Science Fiction Studies* 15 (1988): 214–15; Lorenzo DiTommaso "Redemption in Philip K. Dick's *The Man in the High Castle,*" *Science Fiction Studies* 26.1 (1999): 91–119; Carl Freedman, *Critical Theory and Science Fiction* (Hanover, N.H.: Wesleyan University Press, 2000), 164–80; Laura E. Campbell, "Dickian Time in *The Man in the High Castle,*" *Extrapolation* 33.3 (1992): 190–201; Howard Canaan, "Metafiction and the Gnostic Quest in *The Man in the High Castle,*" *Journal of the Fantastic in the Arts*

12.4 (2002): 382–405; Karen Hellekson, *The Alternate History: Refiguring Historical Time* (Kent, Ohio: Kent State University Press, 2001), chapter 4; Jianjiong Zhu, "Reality, Fiction, and 'Wu' in 'The Man in the High Castle,'" *Journal of the Fantastic in the Arts* 5.3 (1993): 36–45; and Fred Bilson, "The Colonialists' Fear of Colonization and the Alternate Worlds of Ward Moore, Philip K. Dick and Keith Roberts," *Foundation* 34 (Summer 2005): 50–63.

3. For brief introductions to the *I Ching* and to Taoism (and for a discussion of their relevance to the structure and themes of *The Man in the High Castle*), see Warrick, *Mind in Motion*, 44–46. See also Rieder, "Metafictive World of *The Man in the High Castle*," especially 217; and Zhu, "Reality, Fiction, and 'Wu'"

4. This tension between Taoism and fascism is a common theme in criticism of the novel. For instance, Warrick writes: the "richest reading of the novel sees it as an encounter of fascism with Taoist philosophy" (*Mind in Motion*, 40).

5. See *The Man in the High Castle* (New York: Vintage, 1992), 36. All page references are to this edition.

6. Dick has stated that "the SS wrote to all the firms in Germany which had built ovens to make bread, and informed them that they wanted to build ovens to burn up human bodies, and what were the bids on this project, like any commercial project. . . . Not one firm wrote back and said, 'We don't build ovens to burn bodies.' Not one firm." Rickman, *Philip K. Dick: In His Own Words*, 143.

7. See DiTommasso's discussion of this point in "Redemption in Philip K. Dick's *The Man in the High Castle*," especially 101.

8. Aldiss claims that *High Castle* can be "considered as a study of authenticity at every level of existence. . . . Throughout the novel there's an obsession with authenticity" (Aldiss and Wingrove 329). Clareson suggests that the tension between "forgery and authenticity" in *High Castle* is a reflection of Dick's "views on art" (*Understanding Contemporary American Science Fiction*, 161).

9. For a reading of *High Castle* as a commentary on fascism in America and as a statement about how fascism is countered by humanism, see Robinson, *Novels of Philip K. Dick*, 43. For some

commentary on *High Castle* as a treatment of the need for human responsibility in the face of totalitarianism, see Warrick, *Mind in Motion,* 32. For a discussion of the significance of the novel's title, see Warrick, *Mind in Motion,* 58.

10. "For absolute reality to reveal itself, our categories of space-time experiences, our basic matrix through which we encounter the universe, must break down and then utterly collapse. I dealt with this breakdown in *Martian Time-Slip* in terms of time." From Dick's essay "Man, Android, and Machine," reprinted in Dick, *Shifting Realities,* 218.

11. For extended treatments of *Martian Time-Slip,* see Warrick, *Mind in Motion,* chapter 3; Mackey, *Philip K. Dick,* 55–59; Brian W. Aldiss, "Dick's Maledictory Web," in Greenberg and Olander, *Philip K. Dick,* chapter 5; Robinson, *Novels of Philip K. Dick,* 54–60. See also Palmer, *Philip K. Dick,* 154–76; and Andrew M. Butler, "Water, Entropy and the Million-Year Dream: Philip K. Dick's *Martian Time-Slip,*" *Foundation* 68 (Autumn 1996): 57–64.

12. Reprinted in Dick, *Shifting Realities,* 167–74.

13. See Robinson, *Novels of Philip K. Dick,* 80. For an example of the type of criticism that gets bogged down in the seemingly logical absurdities of the novel, see George Turner "Now Wait for Last Year," in Gillespie, *Philip K. Dick,* 46–47.

14. See Rickman, *Philip K. Dick: In His Own Words,* 142–43.

15. "Ethics may far more involve an abstention from evil than a commission of good. . . . All that is being asked is a refusal. No one is being asked to do anything, merely being asked to refuse to do something they shouldn't do. To balk. I define as human that organism that, which when perceiving a threat to its moral integrity, balks." Dick, as quoted in Rickman, *Philip K. Dick: In His Own Words,* 143–44.

16. *Now Wait for Last Year* (New York: Vintage, 1993), 229–30. All page references are to this edition.

17. Dick said of *The Three Stigmata of Palmer Eldritch:* "That was written in connection with my becoming an adult convert to the

Episcopal Church, and my becoming involved in Christianity, and my sense of the reality of the diabolical, which is a carry-over from my prior interest in Zoroaster. For me Evil was as real a force as Good. There was God and there was the Anti-God. It was really a study of Deity as Evil and Good as Human. The good side was human and the evil side was deity. It's like man being confronted with a murderous God. It's essentially a diabolical novel." Dick, as quoted in Rickman, *Philip K. Dick: In His Own Words,* 149.

18. See *Collected Stories,* vol. 4, 377–79, quote on 377; for an account of this vision and this period of Dick's life, see Sutin, *Divine Invasions,* 126–28.

19. All page references are to *The Three Stigmata of Palmer Eldritch* (New York: Vintage, 1991).

20. See the discussion between Barney Mayerson and Anne Hawthorne, 148–49.

21. "It studies different kinds of love and at last ends with the appearance of an ultimate kind of love which I had never known of. I am saying, 'In answer to the question, "What is real?" the answer is: this kind of overpowering love.'" Dick, as quoted in Sutin, *Divine Invasions,* 165.

22. See Rickman, *Philip K. Dick: In His Own Words,* 177–78.

23. All page references are to *Flow My Tears, the Policeman Said* (New York: Vintage, 1993).

24. *Flow My Tears* would later become a very important book in Dick's own estimation. Dick came to believe, in retrospect, that in a passage in *Flow My Tears* he had, compelled by forces outside of his own immediate awareness, encrypted a key (the words *King Felix*) that signaled the beginning of a new period in religious history. He discussed his belief regarding the religious importance of *Flow My Tears* in interviews given right before his death, and it is referred to directly in *VALIS.* For more on this, see Rickman, *Philip K. Dick: The Last Testament,* 202–11. See also *VALIS,* 231. Dick's retrospective interpretation of *Flow My Tears* is part of his larger efforts to try to come to terms with the mystical visions he experienced in 1974.

These visions prompted Dick to write his *Exegesis* and to reconsider his life's work up until that time.

25. "I saw something, and I can remember it very well, but I don't know what it was, what it signified. . . . I'd trade all the rest of my life just to know. I'll never know what it was." Dick, in an interview in 1981, as quoted in Rickman, *Philip K. Dick: The Last Testament,* 51.

26. For an account of this period of Dick's life, see Sutin, *Divine Invasions,* chapter 10. Dick spoke frequently about these experiences in interviews: see Lee and Souter, 147–51, as well as in much of Rickman's *Philip K. Dick: The Last Testament.* Dick explored these events in his *Exegesis* at great length, and many of the relevant passages can be found in Dick, *In Pursuit of Valis.*

27. See Sutin, *Divine Invasions,* 246.

28. The name *Horselover Fat* is a play on Dick's own name: *Philip,* in Greek, means horse lover, while *Dick,* in German means fat.

29. A few passages of *VALIS,* outside of the *Tractates,* were lifted word for word from the *Exegesis.*

30. All page references are to *VALIS* (New York: Vintage, 1991)

31. See *VALIS,* 236–38.

32. See *VALIS,* 69. For more on the cosmology of the *Exegesis* and of *VALIS,* see Sutin, *Divine Invasions,* chapters 10 and 11; see also Rickman, *Philip K. Dick: The Last Testament;* and McKee, *Pink Beams of Light.*

Conclusion: *Apologia pro mea vita*

1. The subtitle of this chapter is taken from the title page Dick constructed for *Exegesis.*

2. *Collected Stories,* vol. 5, 236.

Selected Bibliography

Primary Sources

Novels

Gather Yourselves Together. Written 1950. Herndon: WCS Books, 1994. Mainstream.

Voices From the Street. Written 1952–53. New York: Tor, 2007. Mainstream.

The Cosmic Puppets. Written 1953. New York: Ace, 1957.

Solar Lottery. Written 1953–54. New York: Ace, 1955.

Mary and the Giant Written 1953–55. New York: Arbor House, 1987. Mainstream.

The World Jones Made. Written 1954. New York: Ace, 1956.

Eye in the Sky. Written 1955. New York: Ace, 1957.

The Man Who Japed. Written 1955. New York: Ace, 1956.

The Broken Bubble. Written 1956. New York: Arbor House, 1988. Mainstream.

Puttering About in a Small Land. Written 1957. Chicago: Academy Chicago, 1985. Mainstream.

Time Out of Joint. Written 1958. Philadelphia: Lippincott, 1959.

In Milton Lumky Territory. Written 1958. New York: Dragon, 1985. Mainstream.

Dr. Futurity. Written 1959. New York: Ace, 1960.

Confessions of a Crap Artist. Written 1959. New York: Entwhistle, 1975. Mainstream.

Vulcan's Hammer. Written 1959–60. New York: Ace, 1960.

The Man Whose Teeth Were All Exactly Alike. Written 1960. Willamantic, Conn.: Zeising, 1984. Mainstream.

Humpty Dumpty in Oakland. Written 1960. London: Gollancz, 1986. Mainstream.

The Man in the High Castle. Written 1961. New York: Putnam, 1962.

We Can Build You. Written 1962. New York: DAW, 1972.

Martian Time-Slip. Written 1962. New York: Ballantine, 1964.

Dr. Bloodmoney, or How We Got Along after the Bomb. Written 1963. New York: Ace, 1965.

The Game-Players of Titan. Written 1963. New York: Ace, 1963.

The Simulacra. Written 1963. New York: Ace, 1964.

Now Wait for Last Year. Written 1963. Garden City, N.Y.: Doubleday, 1966.

Clans of the Alphane Moon. Written 1963–64. New York: Ace, 1964.

The Crack in Space. Written 1963–64. New York: Ace, 1966.

The Three Stigmata of Palmer Eldritch. Written 1964. Garden City, N.Y.: Doubleday, 1965.

The Zap Gun. Written 1964. New York: Pyramid, 1967.

The Penultimate Truth. Written 1964. New York: Belmont, 1964.

The Unteleported Man. Written 1964–65. New York: Ace, 1966. Published in expanded form as *Lies, Inc.* in 1984.

The Ganymede Takeover, with Ray Nelson. Written 1964–66. New York: Ace, 1967.

Counter-Clock World. Written 1965. New York: Berkley, 1967.

Do Androids Dream of Electric Sheep? Written 1966. Garden City, N.Y.: Doubleday, 1968.

Nick and the Glimmung. Written 1966. London: Gollancz, 1988. For children.

Ubik. Written 1966. Garden City, N.Y.: Doubleday, 1969.

Galactic Pot-Healer. Written 1967–68. New York: Berkley, 1969.

A Maze of Death. Written 1968. Garden City, N.Y.: Doubleday, 1970.

Our Friends from Frolix 8. Written 1968–69. New York: Ace, 1970.

Flow My Tears, the Policeman Said. Written 1970. Garden City, N.Y.: Doubleday, 1974.

A Scanner Darkly. Written 1973–75. Garden City, N.Y.: Doubleday, 1977.

Deus Irae, with Roger Zelazny. Written 1975. Garden City, N.Y.: Doubleday, 1976.

Radio Free Albemuth. Written 1976. New York: Arbor House, 1985.

VALIS. Written 1978. New York: Bantam, 1981.

The Divine Invasion. Written 1980. New York: Timescape, 1981.

The Transmigration of Timothy Archer. Written 1981. New York: Timescape, 1982.

Philip K. Dick: Four Novels of the 1960s. New York: Library of America, 2007. Comprises *The Man in the High Castle, The Three Stigmata of Palmer Eldritch, Do Androids Dream of Electric Sheep?,* and *Ubik*

Philip K. Dick: Five Novels of the 1960s and 1970s. New York: Library of America, 2008. Comprises *Martian Time Slip, Dr. Bloodmoney, Now Wait for Last Year, Flow My Tears the Policeman Said,* and *A Scanner Darkly.*

Short Stories

A Handful of Darkness. London: Rich & Cowan, 1955.

The Variable Man and Other Stories. New York: Ace, 1957.

The Preserving Machine. New York: Ace, 1969.

The Book of Philip K. Dick. New York: DAW, 1973.

The Best of Philip K. Dick. New York: Ballantine, 1977.

The Golden Man. New York: Berkley, 1980.

The Collected Stories of Philip K. Dick. New York: Citadel Twilight Press. Vol. 1: *Beyond Lies the Wub* (*The Short Happy Life of the Brown Oxford*), vol. 2: *Second Variety* (*We Can Remember It for You Wholesale*), vol. 3: *The Father-Thing* (*Second Variety*), vol. 4: *The Days of Perky Pat* (*The Minority Report*), and vol. 5: *The Little Black Box* (*The Eye of the Sybil*).

Letters

The Selected Letters of Philip K. Dick, 6 vols. Novato, Calif.: Underwood-Miller, 1991–2005. Comprises *The Selected Letters of Philip K. Dick, 1974* (1991), *The Selected Letters of Philip K. Dick, 1975–1976* (1992), *The Selected Letters of Philip K. Dick,*

1977–1979 (1993), *The Selected Letters of Philip K. Dick, 1972–1973* (1993), *The Selected Letters of Philip K. Dick, 1938–1971* (1996), and *The Selected Letters of Philip K. Dick, 1980–1982* (2005).

Other Works and Compilations

I Hope I Shall Arrive Soon. Garden City, N.Y.: Doubleday, 1985. Essays and stories.

Ubik: A Screenplay. Minneapolis: Corroboree, 1985. Screenplay based on novel of same title.

Cosmogony and Cosmology. Worcester Park, U.K.: Kerosina, 1987. Essay.

The Dark Haired Girl. Willamantic, Conn.: Zeising, 1988. Letters, essays, and other writings.

In Pursuit of Valis: Selections from the Exegesis. Novato, Calif.: Underwood-Miller, 1991. Essays.

The Shifting Realities of Philip K. Dick: Selected Literary and Philosophical Writings. New York: Pantheon, 1995. Essays.

What If Our World Is Their Heaven? New York: Overlook, 2000. Interviews.

Secondary Sources

General Introductions to Science Fiction

Harris-Fain, Darren. *Understanding Contemporary American Science Fiction: The Age of Maturity, 1970–2000.* Columbia: University of South Carolina Press, 2005.

James, Edward, and Farah Mendlesohn, eds. *The Cambridge Companion to Science Fiction.* Cambridge: Cambridge University Press, 2003.

Bibliographic Studies

Levack, Daniel J. H., comp. *PKD: A Philip K. Dick Bibliography.* Rev. ed. Westport, Conn.: Meckler, 1988. A comprehensive bibliography of the known published works of Philip K. Dick. Heavily illustrated.

Biographical Studies

Carrère, Emmanuel. *I Am Alive and You Are Dead: A Journey into the Mind of Philip K. Dick*. New York: Picador, 1993. Interesting and provocative to read, but unreliable as biography and overly indulgent with its speculations, Carrère's book is an attempt to tell the life of Philip K. Dick through re-creating Dick's inner life.

Dick, Anne R. *Search for Philip K. Dick, 1928–1982*. Lewiston, N.Y.: Edwin Mellen Press, 1995. A memoir written by Philip K. Dick's third wife, Anne.

Rickman, Gregg. *To the High Castle. Philip K. Dick: A Life 1928–1962* Long Beach, Calif.: Fragments West, 1989. The first installment of a projected multivolume biography. Reads Dick's works closely against his biography. Contains a wealth of interesting information but has been criticized about some controversial speculation regarding certain details of Dick's life. As a biography, however, it is second only to Sutin.

Sutin, Lawrence. *Divine Invasions: A Life of Philip K. Dick*. New York: Carroll & Graf, 1989. Arguably the best of the full-length biographical studies of Dick, with a seemingly even-handed approach to Dick's artistic successes, his failures, and the demons that plagued him. Written with a wit rarely seen in critical biographies. A must-read.

Books on Philip K. Dick and His Works

Brooker, Will, ed. *The Blade Runner Experience: The Legacy of a Science Fiction Classic*. New York: Wallflower Press, 2005. A collection of essays on Ridley Scott's *Blade Runner* (1982), the film adaptation of Dick's *Do Androids Dream of Electric Sheep?*

Butler, Andrew M. *Philip K. Dick*. Harpenden, U.K.: Pocket Essentials, 2007. A useful guidebook to the works of Philip K. Dick, including brief summaries, cross references, and thumbnail analyses.

Clareson, Thomas D. *Understanding Contemporary American Science Fiction: The Formative Period (1926–1970)*. Columbia:

University of South Carolina Press, 1990. An introductory survey of mid-twentieth-century science fiction. Includes treatments of Dick's *The Man in the High Castle, The Three Stigmata of Palmer Eldritch,* and *Do Androids Dream of Electric Sheep?*

Gillespie, Bruce, ed. *Philip K. Dick: Electric Shepherd.* Melbourne: Norstrilia Press, 1975. A best-of compilation of articles and reviews of Philip K. Dick that appeared in the magazine *SF Commentary.* The collection also includes two brief but important letters by Dick, as well as Dick's 1972 lecture "The Android and the Human" and Stanislaw Lem's infamous "Science Fiction: A Hopeless Case—With Exceptions."

Greenberg, Martin Harry, and Joseph D. Olander, eds. *Philip K. Dick.* New York: Taplinger, 1983. Early collection of essays on Dick collected from various sources. Includes the essays by Disch, Suvin, and Warren noted below.

Kerman, Judith B., ed. *Retrofitting Blade Runner: Issues in Ridley Scott's* Blade Runner *and Philip K. Dick's* Do Androids Dream of Electric Sheep? Bowling Green, Ohio: Bowling Green University Press, 1991. A collection of essays dedicated to exactly what the title implies.

Landon, Brooks. *Science Fiction after 1900: From the Steam Man to the Stars* New York: Twayne, 1997. An introductory history of twentieth-century science fiction with treatments of Dick's *Man in the High Castle* and *Ubik.*

Lee, Gwen, and Doris Elaine Sauter, eds. *What If Our World Is Their Heaven? The Final Conversations of Philip K. Dick* New York: Overlook, 2000. A collection of interviews conducted with Dick in the months just prior to his death. Primary topics discussed are *Blade Runner, The Transmigration of Timothy Archer,* his unwritten novel *The Owl in Daylight,* and his attempts to grapple with his religious experiences in 1974.

Mackey, Douglas A. *Philip K. Dick.* Boston: Twayne, 1988. A useful introductory survey of Dick's life and work.

McKee, Gabriel. *Pink Beams of Light from the God in the Gutter: The Science Fictional Religion of Philip K. Dick* New York: University Press of America, 2004. An attempt to sort through Dick's commentary on religion and theology in order to bring some coherence to Dick's evolving religious ideas.

Mullen, R. D., Istvan Csicsery-Ronay Jr., Arthur B. Evans, and Veronica Hollinger, eds. *On Philip K. Dick: 40 Articles from Science Fiction Studies.* Terre Haute, Ind.: SF-TH, 1992. Contains everything on Dick that appeared in the journal *Science Fiction Studies,* including notes and book reviews, between 1975 and 1992. A very useful resource for the Dick scholar. Includes articles by Pagetti, Suvin, Fitting, Freedman, and Philmus cited below.

Palmer, Christopher. *Philip K. Dick: Exhilaration and Terror of the Postmodern.* Liverpool: Liverpool University Press, 2003. A detailed exploration of Dick's works within the context of postmodernism, and as a reflection and exploration of postmodernity. Perhaps not a good point of entry for the general reader of Dick, but it does stand as the most detailed reading of Dick within the context of postmodern theory and fiction.

Pierce, Hazel. *Philip K. Dick.* Starmont Reader's Guide #12 Mercer Island, Wash: Starmont House, 1982. A short introduction to Dick, with extended treatments of four of Dick's best works: *The Man in the High Castle, The Three Stigmata of Palmer Eldritch, Ubik,* and *Flow My Tears, the Policeman Said.*

Rickman, Gregg. *Philip K. Dick: In His Own Words.* 2nd ed. Long Beach, Calif.: Fragments West, 1988. A collection of interviews conducted by Rickman with Dick in 1981. The topics are wide-ranging, but the centerpiece of the volume is a series of conversations in which Dick comments on each of his works in chronological order.

———. *Philip K. Dick: The Last Testament.* Long Beach, Calif.: Fragments West, 1985. A collection of interviews conducted by Rickman with Dick primarily in 1981 and 1982. In this volume, the topics center on Dick's religious visions and beliefs, with special attention paid to Dick's "Tagore" letter, and on Dick's late-in-life views on the imminent return of the Maitreya.

Robb, Brian J. *Counterfeit Worlds: Philip K. Dick on Film*. London: Titan Books, 2006. A history of media adaptations of Dick's works.

Roberts, Adam. *Science Fiction*. New York: Routledge, 2000. A study of science fiction as genre primarily distinguished by its unique use of symbols. Includes a brief discussion of the Marxist concept of commodity fetishization in Dick's *Ubik*.

Robinson, Kim Stanley. *The Novels of Philip K. Dick*. Ann Arbor, Mich.: UMI Research Press, 1984. An influential and important early study of Dick's works. The first study to tackle the complex task of offering a complete critical survey of all of Dick's novels.

Taylor, Angus. *Philip K. Dick and the Umbrella of Light*. SF Author Studies 1. Baltimore: T-K Graphics, 1975. A fifty-page tour through Dick's work with an emphasis on Dick's themes.

Umland, Samuel J., ed. *Philip K. Dick: Contemporary Critical Interpretations*. Westport, Conn.: Greenwood, 1995. A collection of essays on Dick with an emphasis on works that typically receive less critical attention, such as *The Penultimate Truth, We Can Build You,* and *The Crack in Space*. Among the essays reprinted in this volume are those by Freedman, Easterbrook, Wessel, and Palmer cited below.

Vest, Jason P. *Future Imperfect: Philip K. Dick at the Movies*. Westport, Conn.: Praeger, 2007. A study of the various film adaptations of Dick's works.

Warrick, Patricia S. *Mind in Motion: The Fiction of Philip K. Dick*. Carbondale: Southern Illinois University Press, 1987. A thematically arranged treatment of what are generally considered Dick's major works. Themes addressed include the nature of power struggles, madness, world destruction, the nature of good and evil within humankind, the definition of "human," entropy, drugs, and the search for God.

Williams, Paul. *Only Apparently Real.* New York: Arbor House, 1986. A blend of commentary and transcribed interview sessions between Dick and Williams (who later became Dick's literary executor). The interview sessions cover numerous topics, with the central focus on Dick's theories regarding the November 17, 1971, break-in and burglary of his house.

Selected Articles and Book Chapters on Philip K. Dick

Aldiss, Brian W., and David Wingrove. *Trillion Year Spree: The History of Science Fiction.* New York: Atheneum, 1986. A revision of Aldiss's 1973 *Billion Year Spree,* a highly regarded history of science fiction. For an assessment of Dick's role in the history of science fiction, see 329–35 and 408–10.

Broderick, Damien. "Philip K. Dick and Transrealism: Living What You Write." *New York Review of Science Fiction* 11.9 (May 1999): 1, 10–18. Examines the connections between Dick's biography and his "transrealist" aesthetic.

Butler, Andrew. "Science Fiction as Postmodernism: The Case of Philip K. Dick." In *Impossibility Fiction,* ed. Derek Littlewood and Peter Stockwell, 45–56. Atlanta: Rodopi, 1996. On the basis of observations about Dick's belief in the value of the individual as an ethical agent, Butler cautions readers not to too quickly place Dick into the postmodern camp, particularly the Jameson/Marxist/late-capitalist version of postmodernism.

Dick, Philip K. "The Mainstream That through the Ghetto Flows: An Interview with Philip K. Dick." *Missouri Review* 7.2 (1984): 164–85. A wide-ranging interview conducted in 1976 that covers such ground as Dick's views on science fiction and his relationship with the publishing industry.

Disch, Thomas M. "Toward the Transcendent: An Introduction to *Solar Lottery* and Other Works." In *Philip K. Dick,* ed Martin Harry Greenberg and Joseph D. Olander, 13–25. New York: Taplinger, 1983. Originally appeared in 1976 as an introduction to a reprint of *Solar Lottery.* An engaging, readable introductory treatment of Dick's works, with special attention paid to *Solar Lottery.*

DiTommaso, Lorenzo. "Gnosticism and Dualism in the Early Fiction of Philip K. Dick." *Science Fiction Studies* 28 (2001): 49–65. Traces the Gnostic themes that Dick explicitly foregrounds in his later works back to Dick's earliest efforts.

Easterbrook, Neil. "Dianoia/Paranoia: Dick's Double 'Imposter.'" In *Philip K. Dick: Contemporary Critical Interpretations,* ed. Samuel J. Umland, 19–41. Westport, Conn.: Greenwood, 1995. A detailed analysis of the story "Imposter" with an emphasis on the doubling/doppelgänger motif within the story and its relationship to modern theories of alterity or otherness.

Enns, Anthony. "Media, Drugs, and Schizophrenia in the Works of Philip K. Dick." *Science Fiction Studies* 33 (2006): 68–88. Uses contemporary media theory as a means to contextualize Dick's exploration of the merging of media and the conscious mind.

Fitting, Peter. "Reality as Ideological Construct: A Reading of Five Novels by Philip K. Dick." In *On Philip K. Dick: 40 Articles from* Science Fiction Studies, ed. R. D. Mullen, et al., 92–110. Terre Haute, Ind.: SF-TH, 1992. Originally appeared in *Science Fiction Studies* in July 1983. Marxist-oriented treatment of the subjective nature of reality as a central theme throughout Dick's career, arguing that reality in Dick's works is revealed to be an ideological construct. Focuses on the novels *Eye in the Sky, Time Out of Joint, The Three Stigmata of Palmer Eldritch, A Scanner Darkly,* and *VALIS.*

Freedman, Carl. "Towards a Theory of Paranoia: The Science Fiction of Philip K. Dick." In *Philip K. Dick: Contemporary Critical Interpretations,* ed. Samuel J. Umland, 7–17. Westport, Conn.: Greenwood, 1995. Originally published in *Science Fiction Studies* 32 (1984): 15–24. An oft-cited essay in the pantheon of Dick criticism. Building off of Marx, Freud, and Lacan, Freedman develops a theory of paranoia and explains its importance for understanding Dick's works, with special attention paid to the novel *Ubik.*

Gillis, Ryan. "Dick on the Human: From Wubs to Bounty Hunters to Bishops." *Extrapolation* 39.3 (Fall 1998): 264–71. Discussion of the question "what is human?" in Dick's canon, with an emphasis on the role of empathy.

Golumbia, David. "Resisting 'The World': Philip K. Dick, Cultural Studies, and Metaphysical Realism." *Science Fiction Studies* 23.1 (1996): 83–102. Argues for a correspondence between Dick's work and more recent Marxist and poststructurally influenced treatments of the problem of "what is real," and that Dick, as with certain recent cultural critics, participates in a critique of metaphysical realism.

Hayles, N. Katherine. "Schizoid Android: Cybernetics and the Mid-Sixties Novels of Philip K. Dick." *Journal of the Fantastic in the Arts* 8.4 (1997): 419–42. Examines how Dick's work in the 1960s reflects key issues raised in cybernetic information theory.

Hoberek, Andrew P. "The 'Work' of Science Fiction: Philip K. Dick and Occupational Masculinity in the Post–World War II United States." *Modern Fiction Studies* 43.2 (Summer 1997): 374–404. Through a reading of *Time Out of Joint,* this article argues that Dick uses the concept of "work" as a means to comment on postmodern and/or late capitalist culture.

Holliday, Valerie. "Masculinity in the Novels of Philip K. Dick." *Extrapolation* 47.2 (Summer 2006): 280–96. Focusing on *Dr. Bloodmoney* and *Martian Time-Slip,* this article examines Dick's works in the context of contemporary gender theory and sees in them a nascent critique of male crisis in an atomic world.

Hollinger, Veronica. "Science Fiction and Postmodernism." In *A Companion to Science Fiction,* ed. David Seed, 232–47. Malden, Mass.: Blackwell, 2005. Brief overview of the connection between postmodernism and science fiction, with a few thoughts on Dick's participation in both traditions.

Magome, Kiyoko. "The Player Piano and Musico-Cybernetic Science Fiction between the 1950s and the 1980s: Kurt Vonnegut and Philip K. Dick." *Extrapolation* 45.4 (Winter 2004): 370–87.

Reads the image of the player piano as a key symbol of cybernetic themes in Vonnegut and Dick. For Dick, the player piano (or variations thereof) is a symbolic leitmotif of the cybernetic interactions of humans and machine.

Malmgren, Carl. "Meta-SF: The Examples of Dick, LeGuin, and Russ." *Extrapolation* 43.1 (Spring 2002): 22–35. Makes a case for Dick as a leader in creating science fiction that is itself a commentary on science fiction. Focuses on Dick's story "We Can Remember It for You Wholesale."

Pagetti, Carlo. "Dick and Meta-SF." In *On Philip K. Dick: 40 Articles from* Science Fiction Studies, ed. R. D. Mullen et al., 18–25. Terre Haute, Ind.: SF-TH, 1992. Originally appeared in *Science Fiction Studies* in 1975. In a quick survey of Dick's work, Pagetti argues that Dick's challenge of the expectations and conventions of SF constitutes a critique of SF itself; thus, in one sense, Dick writes SF about SF.

Palmer, Christopher. "Philip K. Dick." In *A Companion to Science Fiction,* ed. David Seed, 389–97. Malden, Mass.: Blackwell, 2005. A brief general introduction to Dick's works and themes.
———. "Philip K. Dick and the Nuclear Family." In *Philip K. Dick: Contemporary Critical Interpretations,* ed. Samuel J. Umland, 61–79. Westport, Conn.: Greenwood, 1995. Tours a handful of early stories in order to illustrate the way Dick uses his portrayals of familial relationships as a means of social commentary, especially commentary directed at power relationships.

Philmus, Robert M. "The Two Faces of Philip K. Dick." *Science Fiction Studies* 18 (1991): 91–103. Provides some background and documentary information on the relationship between Dick and the FBI in the mid-1970s.

Rossi, Umberto. "Fourfold Symmetry: The Interplay of Fictional Levels in Five More or Less Prestigious Novels by Philip K. Dick." *Extrapolation* 43.4 (2002): 398–419. A structural analysis contrasting the layers of fictional reality with the layers of real history in *Cosmic Puppets, Time Out of Joint, The Simulacra, The Penultimate Truth,* and *The Man in the High Castle.*

Stilling, Roger J. "Mystical Healing: Reading Philip K. Dick's *VALIS* and *The Divine Invasion* as Metapsychoanalytic Novels." *South Atlantic Review* 56.2 (May 1991): 91–106. Argues that in these two novels, Dick blends ancient metaphysics with modern psychoanalytic theory in order to explore thematically the healing of the damaged human psyche.

Suvin, Darko. "Artifice as Refuge and World View: Philip K. Dick's Foci." In *Philip K. Dick,* ed. Martin Harry Greenberg and Joseph D. Olander, 73–95. New York: Taplinger, 1983. Originally appeared, in slightly different form, in *Science Fiction Studies* in 1975. One of the finest statements on Dick's narrative methodology and an exploration of the phases of Dick's career through 1974. Its focus is on Dick's "multifoci" point of view and its connection to power relationships in his works.

———. "Goodbye and Hello: Differentiating Within the Later P. D. Dick." *Extrapolation* 43.4 (Winter 2002): 368–97. A companion piece to Suvin's 1975 article cited above, focusing on *A Scanner Darkly, Radio Free Albemuth, VALIS, The Divine Invasion,* and *The Transmigration of Timothy Archer.*

Walters, F. Scott. "The Final Trilogy of Philip K. Dick." *Extrapolation* 38.3 (1997): 222–35. Argues that Dick's final three novels are bound by their collective exploration of characters who attempt to preserve psychological wholeness through a reliance on their own consciousness and a fixed (even if false) sense of the real.

Warren, Eugene. "The Search for Absolutes." In *Philip K. Dick,* ed. Martin Harry Greenberg and Joseph D. Olander, 161–87. New York: Taplinger, 1983. Examines the quest for an "absolute" reality in *The Simulacra, The Man Who Japed, A Maze of Death, Galactic Pot-Healer, Now Wait for Last Year,* and "Faith of Our Fathers."

Wessel, Karl. "Worlds of Chance and Counterfeit: Dick, Lem, and the Preestablished Cacophony." In *Philip K. Dick: Contemporary Critical Interpretations,* ed. Samuel J. Umland, 43–59. Westport, Conn.: Greenwood, 1995. Looks at the relationship between paranoia and game theory in Dick's short story "Shell Game" and Stanislaw Lem's *Solaris*.

Youngquist, Paul. "Score, Scan, Schiz: Dick on Drugs." *Cultural Critique* 44 (Winter 2000): 84–110. Focusing on *A Scanner Darkly,* this article looks at Dick's critique of drug culture in America and, in so doing, is itself a critique of drug policy in America.

Index